Both Sides of the Altar

Both Sides of the Altar

Frank Morgan

Introduction by Gerard V. Bradley
Afterword by David S. Morgan

St. Augustine's Press
South Bend, Indiana
2011

Manufactured in the United States of America.

1 2 3 4 5 6   17 16 15 14 13 12 11

Library of Congress Cataloging in Publication Data
Morgan, Frank, d. 2008.
    Both sides of the altar / by Frank Morgan; introduction by Gerard V. Bradley; afterword by David S. Morgan.
        p. cm.
    ISBN-13: 978-1-58731-080-5 (pbk.: alk. paper)
    ISBN-10: 1-58731-080-5 (pbk.: alk. paper)
    1. Priests – Biography. 2. Catholic Church – Clergy – Biography. 3. Catholics – Biography. I. Title.
    BX4705.M68A3 2008
    282.092 – dc22 [B]   2008030710

∞ The paper used in this publication meets the minimum require-ments of the American National Standard for Information Sciences – Permanence of Paper for Printed Materials, ANSI Z39.48-1984.

ST. AUGUSTINE'S PRESS
www.staugustine.net

Table of Contents

Acknowledgments

The author extends his profound and heartfelt thanks to the following family members, friends and associates for their assistance and encouragement.

Father John A. Hardon, S.J., now deceased, who urged me many years ago to set pen to paper and recount the story of my adult life.

David, our first-born son, his infectious enthusiasm supporting my endeavor was a great motivator.

Patrick, our second-born son, his quiet, firm support further added to the successful completion of my manuscript.

Stacey, our daughter-in-law, proofread the original version of my manuscript and generously gave her time and talents to us.

David Stuursma, a remarkable young man, with a keen mind, a sincere heart and excellent insights into my manuscript, was unstinting in his pursuit for excellence.

My dear friend, Hugh McCann, a successful author and former writer for the *Detroit News* and *Detroit Free Press*, to whom I express my sincere thanks for his sage critique, professional advice and, especially for his friendship over the years.

And finally, I extend my heartfelt deep love and gratitude to Ruth, my wife, who labored tirelessly for many hours in assembling the manuscript. Her generosity of time, remarkable retentive memory, excellent insights and suggestions, along with proofreading, were of inestimable value. The title of the book that she kept in her heart for over twenty years, *Both Sides of the Altar*, is attributed solely to her.

Introduction

To begin at the beginning: the invitation to write this Introduction was an offer I could not refuse. It came via an e-mail dated February 22, 2008. The sender was Frank Morgan, a man I had never met but one with whom I shared a dear association. Frank and I were both long-time members of The Fellowship of Catholic Scholars. The Fellowship was founded in 1977 by a handful of scholars who held the faith, whole and entire, as it comes to us through Scripture and the Magisterium. They joined hands to help one another use their intellectual gifts in service to the Church, at a time when faithfulness was scarcely the fashion on Catholic campuses. Frank Morgan did not make his living as an academic. But he had the education and interests necessary to join the Fellowship – and he did.

Among the Fellowship's founders was Father John Hardon, a great Jesuit theologian. He authored forty books, delivered countless lectures around the world, and was closely involved with producing the *Catechism of the Catholic Church*. Father Hardon was a man of extraordinary sanctity, too; he was always a priest, first and foremost. I admired Father Hardon but, unfortunately, never met him either.[1] Shortly after his death from bone cancer in the year 2000, the cause of John Hardon's beatification was opened in Rome by Cardinal Edward Gagnon.

So, when Frank Morgan wrote to me that Father Hardon did not live to write the Introduction he had promised to write – and asked that I do so instead – I did not hesitate to say "yes." Serving as Plan "B" to Father Hardon was an undeserved honor I was delighted to accept.

---

1   You will learn a great deal about this saintly man in *Both Sides of the Altar*, especially in Chapter 16.

Accepting Frank's offer was an easy call for another reason: I had already (by February 22) read Frank's manuscript, and saw that the book had to be published. I was ready to do what I could to bring that about. A short time later, Bruce Fingerhut (and St. Augustine's Press) offered to publish the manuscript. Happily, Bruce concurred in Frank's choice to have me introduce it.

Both Sides of the Altar is, as they say, a "great read." It is a gently told memoir of a boy born during the Depression, a boy who came of age in the golden years of Catholic family life, and a man who lived through the debacle we call the "spirit" of Vatican II. This man lived to tell the tale, too, of today's modest recovery from that disaster. Frank Morgan is not the first author to write in the first person about these eventful years. The actuarial tables show, however, that he will be among the last. And *Both Sides of the Altar* is among the best of the autobiographical accounts we will ever see about twentieth-century North American Catholicism.

The title is meant literally. On one "side" of the altar is the author growing up in a devout Catholic home, serving Mass as a boy, and being ordained a Roman Catholic priest on May 1, 1949. This portrait includes all the *Going My Way* touchstones: Rosary at home, attending a seminary bulging at the seams, serving a bishop who lives in what everyone called "the palace," abiding by the bishop's rule that only black or dark blue autos would do for his priests. Frank even describes a 1972 retreat preached by Fulton Sheen as "the best" he ever heard.

On the other "side" of the altar: Frank Morgan left the priesthood in 1964, not quite part of the wave of such defections across North America in the wake of the Second Vatican Council. The reader can judge how much of Frank Morgan's Catholicism left with him that May 1964 day. By his own account, Frank stopped attending Mass, and drifted away from the Church he had loved and served. He later met and married a non-Catholic woman in a civil ceremony.[2] He found a second career in what we now call "human resources" work.

Through it all Frank retained his Christian faith, attending Catholic Mass (but not receiving communion), staying involved

2   Frank's beloved Ruth was later received into the Roman Catholic Church. Their marriage was also later validated by a Catholic priest.

in social work. And he remained open to Jesus's call. From that May 1964 day forward, our author seems to have understood himself as an *inactive Catholic priest*, one who eventually founded an organization – *Contact* – to help others like himself, as well as active priests who were thinking of leaving. Even then – in the summer of 1967 when the tidal wave of post-conciliar dissent cascade over these shores – Frank and his co-founder Father James McGlynn "determined that *Contact* would be used *only in support of – and in obedience to – the Church.* It would never be used to encourage priests to leave their vocation."

As I write these words I see on television a man much younger than Frank Morgan who has already published two self-congratulatory autobiographies. The man is running for President. *Both Sides of the Altar* comes from the hand of this man's alter-ego: scolded into writing it by Father Hardon, Frank's memoir is free of narcissism and rationalizations of all kinds. The most didactic passage in the book is this dead-on spiritual advice: "The soundness of what we believe absolutely depends upon and is influenced by the soundness of how we live out our moral and spiritual lives."

This memoir is also free of recrimination and score-settling, even with the many still-active priests who treated the (inactive) Morgan as a spiritual leper. Frank heard the news of his father's death in 1967, for example, from his home parish pastor. The pastor took the occasion to instruct Frank not to attend the funeral Mass, and to visit the funeral home only when no one else was around. Though angered and saddened, Frank complied. "It was only many years and much prayer that allowed me to forgive his harsh treatment".

Our author is painfully candid about his own failings. He ascribes his defection from the priesthood mainly to spiritual aridity, which took root in his diminishing zeal in prayer and in ministry. This lukewarmness he attributes squarely to his own self-centeredness. I suppose we should take Frank Morgan at his word: as he increased, Jesus decreased.

Each priest who leaves has, Frank opines in these pages, his own personal reasons. He mentions one such personal reason: the lack of challenges (especially, I should add, for a person possessed of as many gifts as Frank Morgan surely was). And another, which stems from an unexpected plot twist. Frank Morgan counts as the "apex" of the author's priestly life – his "personal Shangri-la" – three years as pastor in Gainesville, Texas. There the young Canadian served as a racial mediator (in tough times: the 1950s). There he started an effective prison ministry. There he acquired a car in off-color! But, he reports, "Gainesville proved to be an important factor in my departure from the Catholic priesthood." Frank Morgan's abrupt re-assignment back to Canada was, evidently, the beginning of the end of his active priesthood.

"Yet, there is a common thread" among the priestly defections. "Even though marriage is most often cited" as the cause, Frank writes in these pages, "loneliness is a greater factor." In a cautionary tale to diocesan priests who typically live alone, he concludes that "priests need priests even more than they realize – not only for recreation but also to share their feelings of loneliness, frustration, discouragement and to seek strength, commitment and consolation as a group in prayer."

Frank Morgan's journey to the Fellowship of Catholic Scholars (and thus to me and this Introduction) began in earnest one day in 1989, the day he read Anne Muggeridge's chilling depiction of Catholic Canada, *The Desolate City*. Frank writes here: "When I finished reading the [Muggeridge] book, I was stunned and angry; stunned at what had occurred because I had been out of touch for many years; and suddenly angry with myself for my immaturity, my laziness, my pride." The book was a wake-up call. He soon got in touch with the Catholic businessmen's association Legatus, worked there for a while, and met Father Hardon in the process. Muggeridge's book was thus the *proximate* cause of Frank's final steps on his journey home to Rome. We can say for sure that Jesus was the efficient cause.

By then Frank was wondering: if the Church *were* to consider married priests, would he return to active ministry? "If I did, how would my priesthood differ from my former lifestyle as a priest? How would priests and laity receive a 'prodigal son' – if such he should be termed." Frank's answers to those questions are the fruits of the spiritual journey recounted in these pages: "These and a score of other questions I've lifted to my heavenly Father. I trust that through His gift of grace the experiences of my life lived on both sides of the altar will ultimately serve the Roman Catholic Church during one of its most tumultuous periods in its 2,000-year-long history."

The main lesson of this important book lies on both sides of the altar. It is that, in season and out of season, Our Lord calls every one by name to help build His Kingdom. There are no exceptions. And Jesus never stops calling.

Catholic faith teaches, and has always taught, that we and everything we do are envisioned by God from before time. The faith has always taught that nothing happens save according to God's will, at least by God's permission. For everything we do is encompassed by God's plan. The implication of these truths is that each of us is somehow involved, in all that we do, in carrying out the work initiated by Jesus Christ, the work of sanctifying the world. Recent Catholic Church teaching is that there is such an organizing principle of the life of each Christian; it is called a "personal vocation."

Pope John Paul II wrote, "What is my vocation means in what direction should my personality develop, considering what I have in me, what I have to offer, and what others – other people and God – expect of me?" Or, in the words of Cardinal John Henry Newman: "God has created me to do him some definite service. He has committed some work to me which he has not committed to another. I have my mission."

One reason that some priests treated Frank Morgan like he had the plague was their impoverished understanding of vocation. During their youth (and during mine, for that matter, two decades later) "vocation" almost always referred to the religious life. Married life was sometimes said to be a calling, but rarely a vocation. Whenever the word "vocation" appeared in the same sentence as the word "family," it meant the possibility that one of the children might become a priest, brother, or nun. Members of the laity had to avoid mortal sin to get to heaven. But beyond that they were to "pay, pray, and obey." Lay men and women had, in other words, no "vocation."

To those scornful priests (and, to some extent, to Frank Morgan) Frank abandoned his vocation for, well, for nothing. This impoverished understanding of vocation has been supplanted in more recent Church teaching by a sounder view less tinged with toxic clericalism. I do not know whether Jesus called Frank Morgan to be an inactive priest, any more than I know whether Jesus called him to be a priest. Or both. I do know, however, that based on more recent Church teaching about personal vocation, it *could* have been so.

*　　*　　*　　*　　*

I said in the first paragraph of this Introduction that I had not met Frank Morgan when I accepted his offer. I never did meet Frank Morgan. His invitation came to me by way of his son David, who attached it to an e-mail message of his own. Dated March 4, 2008, David Morgan's message to me read:

"It brings me great pain and sorrow to inform you of my father's passing on Sunday 24 February, 2008. Two nights before he died he wrote you a letter. My mother and I thought you should receive it."

And so, then, as Frank Morgan neared the end of his race he shared with me some very-nearly final thoughts which I, in turn, share with you dear readers of *Both Sides of the Altar*. I think they express the faith of the man, a faith forged through the crucible of an eventful life lived during tumultuous times, a faith which suffuses each page of this book. Frank wrote to me on February 22, 2008, two days before he died:

> "It has been a constant source of wonder for me to experience the great love of God for all his family, even the wayward. How in His providential care he brings special people into our lives. I think first of all of the beloved Fr. John Hardon and of our warm friendship. He prepared to write the Introduction to *Both Sides of the Altar*, but the Lord had other plans and took him before the manuscript was written. And now God has brought you into my life during my final earthly years. Should it be his Holy Will to have *Both*

Sides of the Altar published, would you kindly consider writing its Introduction?"

This was indeed an offer I could not refuse.

Gerard V. Bradley

Prologue

The following startling words would never have been written in any diocese in the United States from the 1920s to the mid-1960s. Yet the saintly and most gentle priest I have ever known, Father John A. Hardon, S.J., wrote these words shortly before the close of the last millennium:

In 1972 Pope Paul VI said, "Satan's smoke has made its way into the temple of God . . . " Now as we enter the 3rd millennium, it is no longer "smoke" but a raging fire. Catholicism is in the throes of the worst crisis in its entire history . . .

In a nutshell there is one word to describe this devastation – dissent – a disobedient, calculating, deliberate uncoupling, a disassociation, a cleavage, an alienation between the pre-Vatican II church and what has euphemistically come to be called the "Spirit of Vatican II." This massive effort to reform the Roman Catholic Church was the work of perhaps a dozen clerical leaders, bishops and priests, and ten change-oriented nuns. Their motive for declaring their independence from Rome, as well as from the hierarchy, was lifestyle. Rather than reforming themselves from secular, sinful habits, they chose to reform the Church. These dissenters were highly organized and motivated. The results of their unfaithful activities continue with us today, after forty years of wandering in the desert.

These well-trained clergy and religious sisters pursued their progressive agenda of radical change through three institutions: education at all levels, the secular and religious media, and the world of entertainment and celebrity worship. The results over two generations have been abundantly evident. The evangelical virtues of poverty, chastity and obedience were quickly jettisoned, and today are looked on, if not with disdain, as relics of the past now consigned to the dustbin of history. Many of our seminaries influenced by this upheaval began producing priests with a focus on a social agenda devoid of sacramental zeal, respect for authority and the pursuit of personal holiness. In consequence, many Catholic parishes have taken on a business-as-usual, nine-to-five agenda of horizontal rather than vertical activities, causing many Catholics to leave this venerable institution to seek spiritual satisfaction and fulfillment elsewhere.

Some priests, through the grace of God, a minority, to be sure, have sought to maintain their Roman Catholic heritage and identity in spite of obstacles and opposition from hierarchical authority. Due to our pervasive secular materialistic culture, these heroic priests are not always liked but they certainly are respected, even if grudgingly so.

Thus there are two camps in the Catholic Church of today: the socially minded, liberal progressive group and the sacramental, holiness focused group, living side by side in uneasy peace with each pursuing its own agenda.

Oliver Cromwell, the Lord Protector of England, Scotland and Ireland in the 17th century – suppressing my admiration for him has never presented a problem – made an interesting comment on the occasion of sitting for an official portrait: "Paint me, warts and all." His words might be an apt description of what is written here. Father Hardon, whose cause is now up for sainthood, urged me to write this book. This is an attempt to fulfill my promise to him. It is written secondarily to throw some light on our heavenly Father's inexhaustible love for his priests, both fervent and wayward. It is further written in reparation for my selfishness, lack of maturity, hypocrisy, and pride.

ONE

Heaven Slipping Away

Who will ascend into heaven?
> Romans 10: 6

How well I affectionately remember Bishop Kevin Britt, the ninth bishop of Grand Rapids, Michigan. He appeared among us in February 2004, took over full diocesan control in October of that year and died suddenly on May 15, 2005.

He quickly gained the love, respect and loyalty, especially of those priests dedicated to their sacramental ministry. Often when a group of these loyal members of his church would gather to administer the Sacrament of Confession, he would drop in, unbidden, to join them. Afterwards, he looked forward to basking in their fraternal companionship. On one such occasion, as a priest friend told me, Bishop Britt's usual jovial, upbeat manner was overshadowed. Instead, he sat down at the table, put his head on his arm and said, "What am I going to do with my wayward priests?"

His words pierced my ears and joined the cry of my heart – a cry that began decades ago when I was a young man and a wayward priest. Over the next few days, I sat at my desk, prepared my thoughts concerning his question and wrote a letter of introduction and request to meet with him. In a surprisingly short time he replied. He offered me a half-hour window of opportunity to meet with him from 11:00 to 11:30 A.M. His schedule was full to overflowing.

Both of us were right on schedule. These are some of the

qualities I recall during that stimulating meeting. I remember his kindly, relaxed countenance, his intent penetrating eyes, his great listening skills, his incisive questions and his infectious interest.

The assigned half-hour was quickly over and we were only half through my prepared agenda. Bishop Britt immediately canceled his next appointment and we continued to map out ways and means to help his troubled priests. The pieces were beginning to fall into place.

As the hour approached its completion, I felt humbled and encouraged. His final words were, "Frank, I want to get back with you in a few months. Give me time to meet with all of my priests before we pursue our plan." A couple of months later, I was saddened to learn the news of his untimely demise. God's providential ways are not always ours. May his soul rest in peace.

As I write these words, questions begin to run helter-skelter through my mind, one overlapping another. Some I have not considered for a long time. Some I've not stopped thinking about.

I am a priest, one of those troubled ones who turned his back on his priesthood and walked away from his religious vocation and its demanding responsibilities. Why did I become a priest? Why did I desert my priesthood? Does God continue to pursue his priests after their defection, as described in the great classic poem of Francis Thompson entitled *The Hound of Heaven*? How might such men make reparation for their defection?

Each priest had his own personal reasons for his departure. Yet, there is a common thread that ties all of us together. Even though marriage is most often cited as the reason, I suspect that loneliness is a greater factor. In the midst of parishioners where we are called "Father" by all, and so we are, as the conduits of God's sacramental life to them; we are not fathers from a purely physical perspective, and return daily to our rectory room alone with our inner struggles. I am inclined to think that priests need priests even more than they realize – not only for recreation but also to share their feelings of loneliness, frustration, discouragement and to seek strength, commitment and consolation as a group in prayer.

Many of the priests who have left move further away from the institutional church and even begin to attack both its doctrines and practices. Why? Why do some of today's active priests who openly criticize the church, continue to remain within its ranks and enjoy its support? In this vein, why do some bishops tolerate such open non-priestly behavior in their dioceses?

Would I ever return to the active priesthood if circumstances allowed it? If I did, how would my priesthood differ from my former life as a priest? How would priests and laity receive a "prodigal son" – if such he should be termed?These and a score of other questions I've lifted to my heavenly Father. I trust that through His gift of grace the experiences of my life lived on both sides of the altar will ultimately serve the Roman Catholic Church during one of its most tumultuous periods in its 2,000-year-long history.

TWO

Radical Lifestyle Changes

Teach me, O Lord, to follow your decrees;
Then I will keep them to the end
    Psalm 119:33

We rose at 5:30 A.M. to a strident push-button electric bell. Rose, but did not always shine. Just to make sure we were on our feet, a student then rang a hand bell as he walked along the corridors – an exercise to which each of us would be assigned during the year. To the bell ringer's chant of *Benedicamus Domino* (Blessed be the Lord), we would answer (or groan) *Deo Gratias* (Thanks be to God). Our lives quickly became attuned to the twenty-nine bells a day; each peal summoned us to a specific location or activity. Daily early meditation and Mass, study, prayer and recreation were beautifully balanced throughout the day.

St. Augustine's Seminary dates back to the 1920s in Scarborough, Ontario, Canada, overlooking the wind-swept bluffs of Lake Ontario. Its main benefactor was Eugene O'Keefe, the owner of O'Keefe's Brewery. On the day the seminary opened, the local newspaper had a photo of the building on its front page. In place of the actual Cross on top of the imposing copper dome, the newspaper editor substituted an O'Keefe's beer bottle. That was Ontario-Canadian comedy and culture in the 1920s.

During my seminary days in the 1940s, consistently there were approximately 200 students studying for the priesthood. There were no empty rooms in the seminary at any time during those formative years. With few exceptions, the seminarians were real men in the true sense of the word – sturdy, healthy, sincere and single-minded.

My preparation can only be described as seven memorable, warm but challenging years of seminary life. Three of these were devoted to philosophy and four to theology. Our textbooks were written mostly in Latin, a radical and rather scary departure from high school studies.

The abrupt nerve-shattering introduction to this new lifestyle frightened most of us to death during that first week. It was a change proved to make us both humble and mature. A separate room was assigned to each student, with quarters furnished with a desk and an attached bookshelf, a no-spring bed with a decidedly thin mattress, a smooth cement floor with a 36 by 18-inch well-worn rug by the bed, a washbasin and closet. The single window contained a pull-down blind – no curtains were permitted. The Spartans of old never had it so good! Since we were all in the same boat there were no complaints. The lifestyle change was so austere, so daunting that none of us dared to utter a word.

A black cassock and Roman collar were the prescribed dress of the day, except for sports and recreation. The cassock, through daily constant use, often took on a green hue. Though initially cumbersome, within the space of a couple of days, I felt comfortable wearing this floor-length garment.

We were given the first day to unpack, become familiar with our surroundings and greet our fellow budding seminarians.

Our particular class, known as "first philosophers," (a euphemism for such an unlettered group of neophytes) started out with thirty-two aspiring students. During the ensuing seven years of study, six men left to pursue other avenues – from physicians to farmers. Some few, who displayed intellectually superior gifts and related talents, became bishops. Our class produced one archbishop, Leonard Wall of Winnipeg, Manitoba, now deceased. The succeeding class gave the Church two bishops. We wagered that one archbishop was equal to two bishops. A saying making the rounds in those days was that "He who desires to be made a bishop deserves to become one."

No time was wasted. A closed (silent) five-day retreat began that Monday evening. Its purpose, through the instruction of a visiting priest retreat master, was to clarify the essential meaning of the priesthood for us. We were here to be groomed as sacramental, pastoral servants, according to the mind and example of our Lord. We were off and running – from 6:30 A.M. until 9:45 P.M. I recall that the first of our classmates to leave did so at retreat's end. (I met him a few years later while visiting a Jesuit novitiate in Guelph, Ontario, where he was finally ordained.)

Regular routine started the following week.

Did we all meld into one homogeneous lump where our individuality ultimately disappeared? By no means!

It should come as no surprise that the most memorable seminarians are not those with evident intellectual acumen. Those who manifested consistent patterns of goodness, genuine manliness and holiness remain firmly etched in the fibers of my memory. Brilliant as bishops, theologians and sociologists may be today, what we need most are saintly, courageous, down-to-earth, manly, holy bishops and priests!

I remember with admiration my friend Vernon Culleton, who observed the rules of the seminary in both spirit and action. His positive example influenced a great number of us during our years at St. Augustine's. Following seminary, during all the years of his priesthood, he remained unflinching, loyal and steadfast to the Church, in spite of progressive and powerful forces opposing him in the diocese.

These forces became increasingly evident in the 1960s and beyond as a direct result of the so-called "Spirit of Vatican II." The word "dissenters" will occur frequently in subsequent pages. Let's stop here and define its real meaning. Dissent has absolutely nothing to do with theology, either in terms of doctrine or practice. It has everything to do with the acquisition of power resulting from pride that leads to disobedience. In other words, dissent is nothing more than a political device for arousing opposition to sacred authority. *Non serviam* – I will not serve – so declared Lucifer before he was cast into hell. Since he is a seraphim (seraphic angel and leader of the highest order among the angelic choirs), he received only one chance. With human dissenters, wounded both by original and actual sins, we pray they will in all humility come to recognize the authority of the Church they are attempting to destroy. We must always distinguish between Christianity and Christendom – the religion and those who profess to be its followers.

Father Culleton was a model of all that a seminarian should be, coming from a large family where the father was the head of the house and his mother its heart. Both worked together to make their family an authentic "domestic church." Father Culleton was not only obedient to the seminary rules but a bright student who excelled at sports. Baron Manfred Von Richthofen, the most famous of all World War I flying aces, was heard to say on one occasion, "I did not go to war to collect fish and eggs." He was credited with shooting down eighty aircraft. Vernon could well have adapted those words to his approach to seminary life.

His priesthood reflected devotion to Jesus, to his Church and to the parishioners under his care to whom he was a true spiritual father. In his advanced years he retired to a small cottage with severe physical constraints along with his brother, Leonard, also a priest, where they continued to assist in the sanctification of souls.

Joseph Cotter, who hailed from a Canadian maritime province, struggled through the courses of study. Only by the grace of God and his own perseverance pounding the books did he reach ordination. He was a large, ungainly man, friendly to and beloved by all the students. Many years later I inquired about him from a mutual priest friend. He responded, "When Father Cotter walks down the street, little children and dogs follow him." I'm certain that the great St. Francis of Assisi would smile affectionately upon him.

And then there is Vincent Re, my dearest priestly friend. He was older than most when he entered the seminary – a late vocation – a man with a gentle, serious personality devoted to his God, his Church and his flock. God bestowed the gift of Parkinson's disease on him in his later life and it was then that his true sanctity shone forth: his loving acceptance of this cross, with his power of speech reduced to a whisper, the manner in which he celebrated the Holy Sacrifice of the Mass, and his unselfish priestly concern for all. Towards the end of his life he was secretly referred to as "The Saint" among his clerical confreres. He was not a brilliant student, but every day of his priesthood – priest and victim like his Master – his sermons in action spoke volumes.

Vincent was admired for two necessary virtues we all need to possess – charity (both the love of God and the love of neighbor) and humility (realizing the truth about ourselves: which is the acknowledgment that all our talents come from God). These qualities are likened to the high and low notes on a musical instrument. Once we have them securely in place, all other virtues naturally fall into their proper pattern in our lives.

I visited my dear friend Father Re many years after I had abandoned the active priesthood. Unable to live in a rectory due to his illness, he was cared for by his mother and sister in their ancestral home. As I rang the doorbell I wondered how he would greet me. Mrs. Re greeted me like a long, lost son. Then she called out, "Vincenzo, Frank is here!"

A flurry of activity could be heard from upstairs and Father Re appeared on the balcony overlooking the living room. Parkinson's disease had impaired his sense of balance. As he literally tore down the stairs, my heart seemed to be in my mouth for fear that he would fall. Surely, his guardian angel was working overtime. He rushed across the living room and clutched my forearms. Tears glistened in his eyes. "Frank," he whispered, "my dear, good friend! I remember you daily at Mass. If only I had known what you must have been going through, I would have moved heaven and earth to help you save your priesthood."

He treated me with such warmth and Christ-like love. I have often observed that those priests who are genuinely comfortable with their own priesthood had the ability to truly connect with and honor the priesthood in me after I had left the active ranks. By no means did they condone my departure from the priesthood. Instead, they were able to distinguish between, but at the same time join, the priesthood and the person. I have always been uncomfortable with members of the clergy who say to me,

"Leaving the priesthood was not all that bad and there is no need to regret your action." When I began to consider leaving its sacred ranks, I shunned the company of good, solid priests. The world, the flesh and the devil invariably join forces when such an opportunity presents itself. Alone, I was no match for this powerful threesome. Priests need priests like no other group and this is especially true for diocesan priests who daily strive to live in the world but not to be a part of it.

News of the priest-workers of France came to us at St. Augustine's like a bombshell. Without thinking it through, we perceived them as heroic, dedicated men who zealously left their rectories to seek jobs in the factories of France with the objective of evangelizing their countrymen. They lived and breathed in a secular atmosphere. The end result was that the vast majority, over time, abandoned the active priesthood, attempted marriage and joined the ranks of those they sought to sanctify. Being in the world and not of the world requires a delicate balance indeed. Is it any wonder that the great sacramental priest, St. John Vianney, the simple parish pastor in the town of Ars in France is the patron saint of diocesan clergy?

Over the seven years of seminary preparation, I met over 400 men aspiring to the priesthood. No one, to my recollection, ever underwent a psychological evaluation. We were well known in those days by our parish pastors. For the most part we attended daily Mass, regularly went to confession, were altar boys, belonged to the Catholic Youth Organization (CYO), and the Holy Name Society. Psychological evaluations to detect or ferret out character flaws were unheard of. The system itself took care of weaknesses or aberrations. I recall only two seminarians during my seven years of preparation who exhibited homosexual tendencies. Both were asked to leave long before ordination.

Because of my close association with parish activities, the pastor was able to recommend me for seminary to the bishop. I was accepted – I had arrived!

After my ordination to the priesthood, I visited St. Augustine's Seminary only infrequently. On these rare occasions, my soul was flooded with beautiful memories of being close to God and of enduring friendships. My recollections of the

tough, challenging courses, the discipline and the sense of fraternal charity washed over me like large refreshing waves. I always
left with a sense of being spiritually cleansed. If I stood at the
seminary gates today, gazing up at that imposing copper dome,
I am certain those same sentiments would return and prevail.

I must have had an overly sensitive conscience while in the
seminary. I recall on my birthday, during my final year as a deacon, while in the chapel, looking up the Scriptural text for that
day and was horrified to read, "And Judas betrayed Jesus for
thirty pieces of silver."

I was twenty-six years of age when I was ordained to the
priesthood. There were three of us to be ordained in Hamilton
and previous night accommodations were made in the
Cathedral Rectory for this solemn occasion. I tossed and turned
for hours and finally arose from my bed to pace the floor and
pray for most of the night.

The following morning, May 1, 1949, I found myself in the
sanctuary dressed in a floor-length white alb. The bishop and
several priests were present. Other priests would drift in as time
would allow after they had completed their own parish Masses.
Father Vincent Morgan, my uncle, was there front and center,
fairly bursting with pride. The church was filled to capacity with
relatives, friends, and well-wishers. The organ and choir together, offering hymns of adoration and praise to God, blended with
the bells and incense all calculated to focus attention on the purpose of our coming together in this magnificent Gothic cathedral.

During the two-hour ceremony, my thumbs and forefingers
(later to be used for the consecration of the bread and wine) were
anointed with specially consecrated oil, and bound together in
prayerful posture. I prostrated myself on the floor while the
Litany of the Saints was intoned imploring the blessing of the
heavenly hosts upon me. This was the most terrifying moment
of all, as I vividly recall. I was petrified in the realization that the
main ceremony of ordination would immediately follow. This
solemn moment, which still exists today, occurred as the bishop
placed his hands on my head, followed by the priests in attendance similarly performing this centuries-old rite. The terror had

completely vanished by this time and in its place I experienced overwhelming sentiments of peace and joy in my heart. I then received the priestly outer vestments of stole and chasuble and began, in union with the bishop, to recite the Mass prayers. This was my first Mass, concelebrated with my episcopal leader.

Toward the end of Mass, I knelt before him and placed my consecrated hands in his hands. He asked, "Do you promise me obedience?" To which I answered with a simple, "I do."

I can never adequately express the elation that coursed through me as I approached the communion rail after Mass to impart my first priestly blessings on my father, my mother and my three sisters, kneeling there in joyful expectation. (My brother was in India as a Jesuit missionary at that time.) Afterwards, I gave my blessing to the hundreds of people who followed.

The day was filled with joy and good wishes. I would have to be blind and deaf not to realize the immediate transformation that took place. The respect I received, the beautiful comments that were uttered on my behalf. Thank God that we had been repeatedly warned beforehand in the seminary that the adulation was not for the person but for the priesthood, the sublime office in which I had been invested.

That same evening, I found myself at home with my immediate family. My mother, overcome with joy and singing her accustomed hymns in the kitchen, prepared one of her special meals. My three sisters eagerly assisted her. Toward the end of the meal one of my sisters told me that I had a choice to either wash or dry the dishes. This was her way in attempting to keep me humble.

After dinner, as was the family custom, we knelt around the cleared dining room table to recite the Rosary together. My father always, and rightfully, took the lead. As we were about to begin, he paused and asked, "Frank, now that you are a priest, should you not be leading us?" I was stunned and embarrassed. I firmly expressed my refusal, reminding him that he was the head of our household and I was still his son upon whom he and Mother had lavished so much love and support. Dad simply bowed his head and began to pray in his accustomed devout manner.

I thought to myself afterwards, "How easy for a priest to be misled by pride through assuming that he personally was the one deserving of the honors heaped upon him." I tried, time after time, during the years of my active priesthood to remind myself of that fact, that I was merely God's conduit, his pipeline, and often rusty at that.

THREE

Priest Professors, Magnificent Men

The Lord has sworn and will not change His mind:
You are a priest forever, in the order of Melchizedek.
    Psalm 110:4

All our seminary professors, without exception, were priests hand-picked by the bishops for their exemplary lives and scholastic expertise. Monsignor Armstrong, rector of St. Augustine's Seminary, a tall, slim, white-haired, father figure, celebrated the 6:30 A.M. Mass (7:30 A.M. on Thursdays and Sundays because we followed a European schedule). Five times a week he inspired us with the fruits of his meditations on the Masters of the Spiritual Life. The good Monsignor had only one working lung. I can see him now, filling that "single wing" with heavenly energy before exhaling it on the assembly.

Our academic priest-professors, men of holiness and knowledge, challenged us daily with their brilliance as well as their humility. As a body, both teachers and students worked hard and prayed earnestly. We played to win amid the variety of sports in which we engaged. Many of our priest-professors would join us on the baseball diamond and ice hockey rink. Here they played with a similar competitive spirit, as did the seminarians. In this environment, no quarter was asked . . . or given! Each year the local Jesuit seminarians and Christian Brothers were invited to compete with our best baseball and hockey players. We were always able to hold our own with the Jesuits. Year after year the Christian Brothers literally took us apart!

I vividly recall one Brother, a jovial giant of a man. He was six foot, five inches tall, broad-shouldered and fast on his feet. He played defense on their hockey team and took great delight in body checking. He took us out as "clean as a whistle" – never using the boards. On one occasion, a player from our team not only sailed into the boards but right on through them, leaving a gaping hole as he disappeared from sight. Ten seconds later he climbed over the boards onto the ice surface and proceeded with the game. After his frequent body-checks, this huge Brother would roar with laughter, pick us up, usually somewhat dazed, and push us in the opposite direction. We never stood a chance against his team.

Perhaps two incidents best convey the character of our professors. Father James Sheridan was my confessor and spiritual director during those heartwarming seven years. He was born in Ireland and imported his great sense of humor wrapped in a soft Irish brogue. He had an amazing retentive memory and linguistic genius, perfect for teaching Latin and Greek. One evening during the dinner hour, while sitting at the head table with his priestly confreres, a seminarian server accidentally tripped and a freshly baked lemon meringue pie cascaded over the head and shoulders of this Irish priest. Father Sheridan, put his chin in the palm of his hand, thought for a moment, and said, "Why couldn't it have been Corn Flakes?"

While Father Sheridan was a student concluding his theological studies at St. Augustine's (he had arrived as a seminarian), and prior to a final set of written exams, the professor of moral theology announced, "If anyone would care to answer all the questions in classical Latin, I'll give him an extra ten bonus points." Jim Sheridan received a mark of one hundred and ten.

One wintry day, ten years after my defection from the priesthood, I found myself in Toronto with my wife and two young sons. I had thought often during the previous years of Father Sheridan's kindness, inspiration and encouragement. Suddenly I had an over-powering urge to seek him out to say "thank you" before God took him from this life.

Through a couple of telephone calls I learned that he was living in quarters at St. Michael's College, affiliated with the

University of Toronto, as Greek Professor Emeritus. I began to wonder if he would want to speak with me because I had forsaken my priestly duties. The phone call was placed and was immediately answered by a rich unmistakably Irish brogue.

Hesitantly, I uttered, "Father, this is Frank Morgan. How are you?" His immediate warm response quickly put me at ease. "Frank, praise God! Where are you? In Toronto? How often you have been in my Masses and prayers. Please come for a visit right now. These are the directions. I want to see you and to meet your family." His words tumbled out so quickly and his voice was so insistent. How could I refuse this dear man?

I'll never forget the sight as I approached his dwelling on a dreary November afternoon. There he was, well along in age, no longer robust, standing out in the snow anxiously looking at every car that passed, for fear that I might miss the entrance to his modest quarters.

As I left the car to approach him, Father Sheridan pressed forward, grabbing me in a bear-like hug. Ruth, my wife, and our sons, David and Patrick, were also genuinely greeted by this gentle soul. If anything stirs the cockles of my heart, it is the memory of that visit. Whenever I recall the tenderness of his priestly heart, tears fill my eyes.

At that time David, our son, was studying Greek history in seventh grade. Father Sheridan gave him a book on Greek mythology from his extensive library, a book that David continues to treasure to this day. Our discussion in bringing each other up-to-date during that all-too-short visit will always be a treasured event in my life.

Shortly afterwards I learned that he had returned to Ireland, "the land of saints and scholars" – to me he was both – where he breathed his last in the beloved land of his birth. "Eternal rest, grant unto him, O Lord. Let perpetual light shine upon him."

Some ten-plus years later, I again found myself in Toronto. Father Walter Kerr, our seminary English teacher, beloved by all the students in our day, was then retired and living at St. Michael's Cathedral Rectory. To me, he was Canada's answer to the main character in James Hilton's novel, *Goodbye, Mr. Chips.* My phone call to him received a similarly warm response.

Shortly thereafter I found myself sitting in a front room of the cathedral rectory. Father Kerr, then in his early eighties, was still active in parish life. He was especially revered for the hours he spent in the confessional. He told me that Father Lucius Barnett, who had taught canon law during my days in the seminary, was upstairs, permanently confined to bed, suffering severe pain from rheumatoid arthritis and heroically offering it up in reparation for sin in the world.

Our conversation covered many loving recollections of seminary life. Two topics of our conversation remain uppermost in my memory. Gregory Baum, a young, brilliant priest with tremendous potential, following the Second Vatican Council, came under the influence of Karl Rahner and Hans Küng, as well as Charles Curran, to join the ranks of the progressive dissenters – or in the words of the great Father John A. Hardon, "Call them by their true name, heretics."

Father Kerr stated that Father Baum's descent into dissent could have been totally avoided in an easy, direct manner by Emmett Cardinal Carter, Archbishop of Toronto. Father Kerr indicated that a simple telephone call from the Cardinal inviting Greg to join him for breakfast would have sufficed in beginning the process of turning Father Baum around to become a loyal defender of the faith. The Cardinal himself was a brilliant man. Alas, it never happened that way!

In 1974, Gregory Baum, who at that time had left the active priesthood, wrote an article in *Commonweal* entitled, "A Challenge to Love: Gay and Lesbian Catholics in the Church." This is considered a ground-breaking event in the emergence of gay activism in the Church. For Canadian Catholics, Baum, a *peritus* (expert theologian) to the Canadian bishops at Vatican II, is the man most responsible for the corruption and collapse of Canadian religious life in the era following that Council. Again, what a tragedy that Cardinal Carter had not paid more attention to his priest protégé!

The second memorable topic involved a young priest from my home diocese, Father Lawrence Howcroft. He was an outstanding scholar and athlete with a personality to match. "Future bishop" was written all over him. During the years following his ordination, he also defected. Unfortunately, a priest with excessive zeal treated him harshly, unjustly and uncharitably. It was the catalyst that turned Father Howcroft away from orthodoxy to a decidedly liberal progressive stance. How different from the treatment I received from Fathers Sheridan and Kerr, and later, from the great Father John Hardon.

As I reflect now on my visit with Father Kerr, respect for our mutually shared priesthood permeated our conversation. At the time of my departure, I asked him for his blessing; afterwards, he knelt down and asked me for mine. It was a humbling, tearful moment, never to be forgotten.

In my later years of association with Father John Hardon, he, too, manifested the same recognition for the sacred priesthood that we both shared. At the end of our private meetings and telephone conversations, he would invariably give me his blessing and then ask me for mine.

These occasions always reminded me of my priesthood and of God's expectations due to the graces given to me. The thought sometimes occurs to me – should I attain my eternal salvation – how will my priesthood, upon which I turned my back, be celebrated in heaven? Oh, if only Father Hardon were still with us in his bodily presence to discuss this topic with me!

During my final seminary years, the first television set found its way into the priest-professors' common room located across and just down the hall from the chapel. Not all of the priests found it particularly attractive but a few eagerly made their way after the six o'clock evening meal to view the news and, perhaps, one or two innocent programs. In retrospect we are now aware of the cultural devastation occasioned by television. I idly wonder if this was the proverbial nose of the camel or the snout of the snake into the tent of the priesthood. After all, how could Howdy Doody possibly be dangerous?

In looking, therefore, for a place, person or event on which to place blame for my defection, it was certainly not the seminary.

But how things have changed in the seminary since my time there! In August of 2001, I received a form letter from the President of Catholic Extension. It was a request for financial assistance. The letter took the form of a scare tactic. Let me sum-

marize its content: What if – there was no priest to celebrate
Sunday Mass in your parish, or baptize your child or grand-
child, or hear your confession, or perform a marriage, or anoint
the sick? He continues, "America is running out of priests." His
letter attempts to enlighten us to the fact that in poor parishes in
rural mission churches men are yearning to become priests but
are prevented due to lack of funds. He informs us of the
astounding fact that the yearly seminary cost is over $15,000 a
year and states, without equivocation, "If you don't help, it
could be your church that one day has no priests."

To state that a lack of funds is the cause of the dearth of vocations is shortsighted in the extreme. Saintly courageous bishops
lead to holy priests who, in turn, lead to devout lay people that
result in an increase of religious vocations and adequate financial support. If the bishops of this country would listen to, and
then visit, their episcopal confreres in whose dioceses vocations
are plentiful and earnestly put into practice what they have
learned, the shortage problems would disappear.

In all truth, I have thought more than once that many of the
bishops in our country are losing touch with reality. They appear
blinded to the fact that no longer do eighty percent of Catholics
attend Mass regularly on Sundays. Today, the figure most quoted is closer to twenty-five percent.

Many episcopal leaders enjoy comfortable lifestyles. Many
live in privilege. Many are catered to purely because of their
position and as a result are often insulated and pampered. By no
means does this apply to all of those who have received the plenitude of priestly powers. With gifts of upscale cars, special personal monetary offerings, meals and accommodations, full
health insurance coverage, vacations, overseas travel and often
memberships in a local country club, is it any wonder they sense
no problem spending other people's money – sometimes with
abandon? Both accountability and common sense are lacking in
such lives.

Is it too much to expect our clergy to live modestly in imitation of Christ?

In my humble opinion, at least once a year every diocesan
priest and bishop should read or reread a book and prayerfully

ponder the life of St. John Vianney, parish priest of the obscure town of Ars in France. The Cure of Ars is the patron saint of all parish priests. His humility, poverty of spirit and total focus on the sacramental nature of the priesthood should inspire all members of the clergy, both bishops and priests, to use his life as a yardstick in their own pursuit of personal sanctity. For an easy down-to-earth read, Henri Gehon's *The Secret of the Cure of Ars*, is an excellent and inspiring introduction to the life of St. John Vianney.

FOUR

The Way a River Runs

Fear God and keep His commandments,
For this is the whole duty of man.
For God will bring every deed into judgment,
Including every hidden thing,
Whether it is good or evil.
        Ecclesiastes 12:13–14

The first parish of my priesthood was a summer assignment at the Cathedral of Christ the King in Hamilton, Ontario. There I was taken in tow by the pastor and senior assistants. A confessional was assigned to me; a priest was with me as I carried out the ceremonies of Baptism for the first time. Baptisms took place at 3:00 P.M. every Sunday afternoon. A priest accompanied me on my first Anointing of the Sick. My first sermons were critiqued before actual delivery on Sunday mornings. The priestly camaraderie was great!

I found out soon enough why I was given this summer assignment. Bishop Ryan, whose residence, referred to as "the palace," was separate from the rectory on the far side of the cathedral. Like the rest of his priests, he took his turn hearing confessions on weekends. A couple of times a week he would send a message summoning me to headquarters. Time to exercise his sturdy arm for half an hour. It was my responsibility (under obedience) to be the pass receiver. He threw a good accurate spiral. Football was one of my favorite sports.

I remember an incident some years later in another parish

when a clerical friend and I arranged for earlier than usual Sunday afternoon baptisms. Afterwards, we sped to Toronto, some fifty miles away, to watch a Canadian Football League game from the bleachers. My friend began to titter to himself until I asked him why. By the way, we were dressed in our clerical attire. He replied, "If only the bishop could see us now!" A few seconds later we heard a familiar voice from the row behind us saying, "Good afternoon, Fathers." It was our own Bishop Ryan! He took our presence in good humor.

In his later years, shortly before his retirement, this same bishop opposed the majority of his episcopal (bishop) confreres who, in their rejection of *Humanae Vitae*, sought to give primacy of place to individual consciences rather than obedience to the Church. (*Humanae Vitae* is the great watershed encyclical, the papal letter of Pope Paul VI, on marriage – its purpose and its pitfalls.) This meeting became known as the infamous "Winnipeg Statement," when the Canadian bishops allowed their authority to be usurped giving individual judgment authority over the teachings of the Church that Jesus had established. Recall his words, "the gates of hell shall not prevail against it" (Matthew 16:18). Its hierarchical authority, then, is not a human construct; it comes from the Son of God Himself.

In the mid-1970s I had left the active priesthood behind for several years. My heart filled with admiration for Bishop Ryan upon learning that, in his eighties, he stayed up until 2:00A.M. in defense of the faith. He lived into his early nineties, cared for by the Sisters of St. Joseph in their infirmary. Visits to him were severely restricted as were telephone calls.

One sunny spring day when all seemed right with the world, while visiting my mother and sisters in Hamilton, Ontario, I placed a phone call to my aged bishop. I was promptly informed that he had given strict orders to the religious sisters to limit his personal calls. I asked the convent operator to mention my name to him. A moment later I heard a voice with severe overtones, "Are you still a Catholic?" This was his opening gambit. I sensed the anger in his voice as I jokingly replied: "You haven't mellowed a bit. Yes, I am still a Catholic, how about you?" I thereupon told him about my concern for his failing health and then apologized for the pain I had caused him and asked for his blessing. I could feel his anger fading away. We chatted for a while about our mutual priest friends. Finally he said, "I'm so happy you called, Father." (Yes, he called me "Father.") Please call me the next time when you are in town." He died before my next visit to the city of my birth.

In the autumn of 1949 I received my first real assignment to a city some forty miles away. Originally the city was named Berlin, since the people were eighty percent German. During World War I the name was officially changed to Kitchener. The pastor at St. Joseph's was in his sixties, a man of boundless energy and priestly dedication. He was known to be a taskmaster but we worked well together. Why? He asked of me nothing he was unwilling to do himself. Years later, someone pointed to him as the cause of my departure. I shook my head in wonderment. The cause of my defection was in me, not in the Church, or in any priest or bishop.

There was no lack of priestly duties in a parish of over 700 families. I was regularly scheduled to celebrate the 7:15 morning Mass. Confessions were always heard before every Mass. After Mass, following an adequate thanksgiving, I would return to the darkened confessional for half an hour or up to the beginning of the Canon of the 8:00 Mass. Since sizeable numbers of students were present, along with many adults, both pastor and assistant distributed Holy Communion at the altar rail to kneeling participants. An altar boy would accompany each of us with a gold-plated paten held under the chin of each communicant to guard against the Sacred Host falling to the ground.

Regarding Confessions: Why today are we told at Catholic religious gatherings that Confessions will be heard *after* Mass? Children are to make their first Confession prior to their first Holy Communion. Why, then, this apparent inconsistency? If indeed extra time is required for Confessions, then, by all means, Confessions should be heard after Mass for those unable to confess beforehand. We heard Confessions seven days a week before Masses, plus two Saturday sessions (afternoons from 3:30 to 5:00 P.M. and from 7:30 to 9:00 P.M.), with both priests in their confessionals and constant lines of penitents.

The Way a River Runs   23

Both Scripture and Tradition unequivocally teach us that Jesus instituted seven Sacraments as the chief conduits of grace won for us by His passion and death. They actually follow us from birth through Baptism to final anointing when in danger of death.

Confession, the Sacrament that removes sins committed after Baptism, does not operate like microwave – two minutes and you're done. There are certain necessary conditions on the part of the penitent for its validity, not only to cleanse us but also to heal us. These include: a proper and thorough examination of conscience, a genuine sorrow for our selfish transgressions against God and His laws, the actual telling of our sins both in kind and in number to a priest in Confession and a firm determination to amend our lifestyle. In other words, the sinner must make a personal decision to confront the evil and sin in his life and make a firm commitment to do something about it. It is only then, as the confessor pronounces the words of absolution, that the penitent is showered with God's grace. The formula of absolution is instructive as the priest raises his hand over the penitent:

God, the Father of Mercies, through the death and resurrection of His Son has reconciled the world to Himself and sent the Holy Spirit among us for the forgiveness of sins; through the ministry of the Church may God give you pardon and peace, and I absolve you from your sins in the name of the Father, and of the Son, and of the Holy Spirit.

Describing the graces one receives in Confession, no one has said it better than Pope Pius XII, one of my all-time favorite holy fathers. Listen closely to his words:

Through frequent Confession, genuine self-knowledge is increased, Christian humility grows, bad habits are corrected, spiritual neglect and tepidity are resisted, the conscience is purified, the will strengthened, a salutary self-control is obtained, and grace is increased by virtue of the Sacrament itself.

Adding to these words, the great and beloved Father John Hardon wrote the following in the mid 1990s:

The Pope [Pius XII] wrote these words in 1943. In the light of what has happened I consider his strong defense of frequent confession prophetic. We shall not restore the Church to her former glory and, please God, to a more glorious future until we bring back frequent Confession.

By the way, after the death of Pope Pius XII the rumor was leaked by some of his enemies, who had a hatred for the Catholic Church, that he was soft on Hitler during World War II and was referred to as Hitler's Pope. The rumor was quickly snapped up as fact by the secular media and word spread. It was then that the Vatican opened its archives and invited researchers in for public scrutiny. It was found that this much-maligned Pope had actually saved the lives of some 870,000 Jews. He had them hid throughout the Vatican and Rome in convents, monasteries and rectories as well as in the homes of devout Catholics who put themselves in danger of imprisonment and death.

Is it any wonder, therefore, that after the war Golda Meier and Albert Einstein visited Pope Pius XII to personally express their heartfelt gratitude? Further, the Chief Rabbi of Rome became a convert to Catholicism.

A pastor of a large church near my home in Grand Rapids, Michigan, hears Confessions in a brightly lit, squared-off area in the rear of the church with a large picture window. Priest and penitent (few they are) are clearly visible as they "chat" face-to-face. As parishioners proceed to their pews, they cannot help but observe this tableau. Is this a priest confessor or a priest psychologist? Confession should include two factors: availability and anonymity. St. John Vianney, where are you? You are sorely needed today! We implore your intercession for our sometimes blind, beleaguered priests. Following your example, may they, through their preaching, arouse awareness among their parishioners concerning sin and its devastating effects. Please, God, may our priests once again spend time daily in a closed, secured confessional.

Another parish activity assigned to me at St. Joseph's in Kitchener included chaplaincy of a large, local tuberculosis sanatorium. Tuberculosis, a serious and sometimes fatal respiratory disease, has all but been eliminated today. On Friday afternoons, both the head pastor and I visited these patients, some of whom were confined to their quarters for months and sometimes for years. All patients, regardless of religious affiliation, received a visit. Those not Catholic welcomed us warmly as dear friends. I celebrated Mass at the hospital once a month with Confessions for an hour before Mass. Since tuberculosis was then considered so infectious, the patients would sometimes ask if I was concerned about catching it. In all truth, it never was a fear. In good humor the patients spoke of forming a reserve army brigade, ready at a moment's notice, to march forth and breathe on any enemies who might threaten to invade our shores.

Like clockwork, both pastor and assistant visited weekly each classroom in our parish school to review the previous week's catechism lesson. We were blessed with a convent of devout, dedicated sisters ever faithful to their teaching apostolate. The Novena to our Lady of Perpetual Help, a popular Catholic devotion consisting of special intercessory prayers, was held regularly at 7:30 on Friday evenings, followed by Benediction of the Blessed Sacrament. The priest at the Benediction ritual blessed the congregation with the Sacred Species contained in a gold-plated reliquary. There was always a large crowd of parishioners who participated with great reverence and devotion. It goes without saying that Confessions were heard immediately afterwards.

Even as I write I hear the sounds of those beautiful hymns, *O Salutaris* and *Tantum Ergo*, while the aroma of incense ascends heavenward permeating the air. These devout Catholics never heard of "active participation" as spelled out in the first Vatican II documents. However, they certainly lived out the authentic meaning of those words, through "engaged" participation by their attentive focus at Mass and during these weekly parish devotions. A sense of the sacred impacted all the senses: sight, sound, smell and hearing. In the early 1950s an estimated 75 to 80 percent of all baptized Catholics attended Mass every Sunday and on all eight Holy Days of Obligation. People today will argue, "Sure, they had time for it then!" I answer, "Where my treasure lies, there too is my heart." Re-education for a change of heart and priorities is desperately needed today. We have so many fleeting creature comforts and labor-saving devices that an inordinate amount of time is spent in pursuing them, cleaning them or commiserating that the newer model is that much better.

Parish organizations included the Holy Name Society for men, the Catholic Women's League and the Catholic Youth Organization. A priestly presence at these activities was the norm. Those interested in receiving instructions in the Catholic faith received a series of solid, individual, systematic lessons, each one leading logically to the next lesson, from either the pastor or his associate pastor. Today, these instructions are much too frequently unfairly placed by the parish priest on the shoulders of parishioners with little training for this important work. It is easy to understand how such lessons can lead to a limited, confused or misleading concept of Church doctrine and practice for sincere seekers of truth, in spite of the eagerness and dedication of the lay instructors to do a good job.

Interestingly, in bygone days there were no lay activities described as "ministries." People had an instinctive awareness of the essential distinction between the priestly ministries and the apostolates of the laity. Today, there is a significant blurring of these distinctions that I find disturbing. We have ministers of hospitality, youth ministers, hospital ministers, music ministers, prison ministers, and even now, card ministers, all conducted by lay persons whose real work is to involve themselves with apostolates – not ministries. Only priests and deacons, along with a few truly required laypersons, conduct ministries around the altar.

The Decree on the Apostolate of Lay People stemming from Vatican Council II states that the distinct role of the laity is essentially in society. Through spiritual formation and preparation from both bishops and priests, they are to act as leaven in their homes (domestic churches), in their places of work and in the community in which they live by their word and especially by their Christ-like example. Those with special God-given talents should offer their talents to the diocesan bishop and to their parish priests in such areas as: finances, legal matters, medical, environment, construction, engineering and civil enterprises. Regularly and at least weekly, they return to their parish church to recharge their spiritual batteries. Refortified and reinvigorated, the lay apostles take their proper place in their community to do battle with the forces of evil in an often inhospitable, secular humanist environment. Thus, a priest, by virtue of his ordination, in true fatherly fashion confects and confers the needed sacramental graces while spending himself as a pastor and teacher while keeping his feet on the ground and his vision on heaven. Lay people, by virtue of their baptism and confirmation, belong to the priesthood of the laity. Like Gunga Din, the water carrier, they bring the sacramental graces they have received to Christianize the culture in which they live, work and have their being. The trick is to maintain a proper balance after contemplating the ideal.

By far the most effective apostolate in our parish, the Legion of Mary, met regularly like an army in battle array to pray for Divine assistance through Mary's powerful intercession before the throne of her Divine Son. The final words spoken by Mary in the Scriptures are found in the story of the Marriage Feast at Cana, "Do whatever He tells you" (John 2:5). As parishioners were repeatedly instructed, "If your devotion to Mary does not lead you to her Son, then there is something wrong with your devotion." The work of the Legion bore abundant good fruit. A significant number of the twenty-five to thirty percent of lapsed Catholics in the 1950s and early 1960s returned to the practice of their faith through the prayers and works of the Legion's devout, dedicated members.

It further fell to the assistant parish pastor to fill his spare time by visiting the homes of his parishioners. The number of small and large problems discussed and solved, with the inspiration of the Holy Spirit over a cup of coffee at the kitchen table, is lost in the mist of time. Invariably, priests received a friendly welcome even from those estranged from the practice of their faith over long periods. It was the priesthood they were honoring, not the man who had been given this sacred gift.

I also had a "housekeeping" activity bestowed on me by the pastor. Every Saturday morning at 5:00 A.M., I drove our aged German housekeeper and accomplished cook, Gertrude, to the downtown Farmer's Market. Invariably, I would park in a lighted area near the front entrance – plenty of parking in the wee hours of the morning. I would then begin praying that day's Divine Office, beginning with *Matins* and *Lauds*.

The Divine Office is a serious priestly obligation to offer daily praise to God in the name of busy parishioners intent on secular duties to support their families and themselves. During this Saturday early morning time of prayer, the only distraction was the steady clip-clop of horses' hooves pulling the Mennonite buggies to market. The dark was lit by the candle lantern attached to the rear of these carriages. It was common practice among most priests to get an early start on the Divine Office since it took about an hour a day to complete. In that way, in the midst of a busy schedule, the *Opus Dei* did not become the *Onus Diei* (the work of God did not become the labor of the day). That one may take a bit of pondering!

In those days, there was no concept such as that of nine-to-five office hours for priestly work, as is found today in too many parishes. Our day began about 6:00 A.M. and usually finished around 9:00 P.M. Emergency sick calls in the middle of the night were not uncommon. There was a single concession to our schedule, no doubt due to a European influence – a one-hour siesta following lunch – a most civilized custom. "Burned out" was not a part of our clerical lexicon.

As first-year priests we were not allowed to purchase a car for one year following ordination. Our particular bishop at that time had a hard and fast rule that stated the color of the vehicle for all priests, without exception, had to be either black or dark blue. I learned to drive at the ripe age of twenty-six or twenty-seven, shortly before I made my first car purchase. It was a bus driver, Don Haefling, a parishioner, who patiently struggled to instruct me.

God's providence works in all sectors – both religious and secular. The first person I instructed and brought into the faith, with God's grace, was a first-class auto mechanic. He gave the car I had bought – a dark blue, second-hand 1947 Chevrolet – a complete inspection and quickly pronounced it a lemon. Ultimately, he found a better vehicle for me – a 1946 Chevy, also dark blue.

On one occasion the bishop remarked that the purpose of

having a car was not only to get around the parish but also to get the priests out of the parish. We would strive to take a day off each week, one day only, but only after hearing Confessions and offering up morning Masses. We took these occasions to visit with both family and clerical confreres. The diocesan stipulation was to be back in the rectory by 11:00 P.M.

Some years ago I stopped in London, Ontario, to have lunch with Bishop John Sherlock, now retired. We had been seminarians together; he was in the class one year behind mine. As we reminisced, he remarked, "Let's face it, Frank, we were far busier priests than they are now." I'm inclined to agree.

It was a busy schedule, to be sure, but no more so than those of our devout parishioners raising families and working to make a living. Besides, we had a secret weapon – proximity to our Lord in the Blessed Sacrament. Here was centered the very source of our dedication, strength and focus. In those days, churches were unlocked from morning until evening. It was a rare moment, indeed, that a church was empty. Daily visits were the norm for many parishioners. In some intuitive way, unlike today, the vast majority of our Catholic people had no thought of changing the form of worship or of deforming the good soil of the Church and her Sacraments. Rather, they did understand the need to constantly renew and reform their own hearts to better receive the seeds of Divine Grace.

Much of this insight came from the practice of frequent Confession, where they also received practical spiritual direction. A deep interior change (*metanoia* – Greek word for interior change) enabled us to turn more fully toward the imitation of the humanity of Jesus in order to increasingly participate in His Divinity. Unfortunately, the euphoria that accompanied Vatican Council II drowned out this message of interior conversion. For the most part, it went unheeded and, finally, almost disappeared. In place of an interior effort by each individual striving continuously to transform the human heart, the focus shifted to changing the external functions of the Church.

A quote attributed to Abraham Lincoln fits the situation eloquently: "The reason why a river runs crooked is because it takes the path of least resistance."

FIVE

A Prodigal Son
Leaves the House of His Father

"Woe to me!" I cried. "I am ruined!
For I am a man of unclean lips,
And I live among a people of unclean lips,
And my eyes have seen the King,
The Lord Almighty."
   Isaiah 6:5

In the 1950s Archbishop Fulton J. Sheen, a popular radio and television personality, and a voluminous writer, made a number of visits to our diocese to speak at a well-attended Catholic Culture Series. He usually stayed overnight at St. Patrick's rectory. On the evening before his speaking engagement, he gathered with a number of parish priests for dinner and for what is often described as a clerical bull session – a combination of light banter and theological lore. On one of these occasions a difference of opinion over an obscure theological principle developed between the then-Monsignor Sheen and one Father Corbet Warren. The issue went unresolved.

Before he retired for the night, Sheen researched the point at issue from the well-stocked parish library. Satisfied with his findings, he gently knocked on Father Warren's door. When the priest answered, Monsignor Sheen declared, "Father, you were right and I was wrong. Please give me your blessing before I retire for the night!"

In the 1940s Monsignor Sheen came to the rescue of a very troubled priest. The story has never been made public, but came to me from the lips of the priest himself. This priest, Joe, had left the active ranks of the clergy in an era when that was considered by most as an unpardonable sin, a most serious scandal, and the cause of great consternation.

Many years later, after my own defection, I visited Joe in a Canadian border city adjacent to Detroit, where he lived with his wife, Ethel. Both of them had been reconciled to the Church for many years. They were devout Catholics who were daily Communicants and Mass-goers, even though Joe's health was failing.

Years previously Joe and Ethel had been hounded and pilloried by well-meaning but imprudent members of the Church who, in their excessive zeal, brought them great harm, suffering and poverty. One attempt was made to kidnap Joe and force his return to the priesthood, while his wife was threatened with accusations of prostitution and with jail. Joe told me his story with the promise that it be kept secret until both he and his wife died. Both of them have passed into eternity, along with Archbishop Sheen, so the story can now be recounted.

Someone brought word of Joe and Ethel's plight to Monsignor Sheen, who was Director of the Society for the Propagation of the Faith in the United States. By this time the hapless couple had fled to Florida in order to escape further persecution. Assisting such "renegades" – a most uncharitable term used to describe them – was severely frowned upon. The merciful monsignor quietly sent them checks month after month to sustain and comfort them until they were able to stand on their own financial feet. I hope and pray that by now they have greeted one another in joy and gratitude in God's celestial kingdom; however, I continue to pray for the repose of their souls.

In 1972, Archbishop Sheen preached a retreat to the priests and seminarians at Holy Trinity Seminary at the University of Dallas. His words were made available on the audiotapes, "Retreat For Priests," by Bishop Sheen. It is my humble opinion that every bishop, priest and seminarian should prayerfully and attentively listen to the tapes. I regard the retreat he preached as the best I have ever heard.

Of special interest to an inactive priest, like myself, was his topic: "Why Priests Leave." Did he really have an answer to which I could affirmatively respond? It was not an answer – it was *the* answer! The good Archbishop was right on target – right in the center of the bull's eye. He told the priests and seminarians assembled that day in the chapel that lack of devotion towards our Lord in the Blessed Sacrament was the essential factor in priestly defections.

His words forced me to examine my own priestly behavior prior to leaving the priesthood after fifteen years. It became crystal clear that in parish activities, increasingly I was spending more time on horizontal rather than on vertical pursuits – the quasi-secular over the solidly sacred. I was still celebrating Mass with devotion. I was still properly and prayerfully administering the sacraments of Confession, Baptism, Marriage and Extreme Unction (Anointing of the Sick), and I was daily reciting the Divine Office – but with gradually diminishing fervor, increased distractions, often hurriedly late at night, rushing its completion before the midnight deadline.

In essence, I became too busy serving others, less inclined to adore and implore our Lord and Savior. I had become indispensable to others, so I blindly thought, one of God's great gifts to the little world I inhabited. My daily Holy Hours imperceptibly diminished until they all but disappeared.

Whatever feelings of guilt I experienced, I attempted immaturely to squelch through frequent appeals to my indispensability. I was so busy serving other causes that, in my pride, I thought I alone could handle. How foolish to think that no one could possibly do what I could do, or do it as well. The world, the flesh and the devil – power, pleasure and possessions – were gradually taking over my life as his satanic majesty covered my eyes with a blindfold leading to an ever-increasing darkness.

Today, as I force myself to look back at those tragic days of my priesthood, I shake my head in wonderment at my stupidity, selfishness and short sightedness. If, in these pages, I appear to cast aspersions or condemn others in the priesthood, then, in all truth, justice and humility place me front and center among those who should stand accused.

Then, in the depths of my soul-searching and despair, a remarkable thing happened. A priest friend noticed that I was gradually pulling away from other priest associates. With sincere, good intentions (I learned this years later), he approached the bishop with his concerns. Thus, it was that the bishop informed me of the parish in Gainesville, Texas, that needed help. He surmised (without sharing this information with me) that a total change might turn me around. Under promise of obedience to him, I was soon on my way.

Most of us have our own secret garden, a personal Shangri-la. This place, either real or imagined, can be visited in a twinkling of an eye. Especially in times of stress and trouble this personal Eden becomes a haven from storm-tossed emotional upheavals. I continue to visit my own inner sanctum, as I have done on countless occasions, when I perceive life to be harsh, unjust or unfair. It pervades my soul with a sense of peace through God's mercy.

My secret space is not a figment of my imagination but a real place in Texas. Some seven miles from the southern border of Oklahoma and seventy-five miles due north of Dallas; it is the town of Gainesville, and in my thoughts I often return there.

My dear friend, Father Bill Lane, the only black Catholic priest in the diocese of Dallas, was the pastor of a poor black parish around the corner from St. Mary's Church in Gainesville. Early on we formed a strong brotherly friendship. I found myself depending on his gentle strength, his wisdom and his goodness. Apparently, he felt similarly towards me. At the end of one of his frequent visits to the rectory, as he sat on the stairs in the hallway entrance, he remarked, "Frank, I am convinced that God sent you here for a special reason. You are the only person in this entire town with whom I can open up my heart and express how I really feel. Thank you for being my dear brotherly friend in Christ."

Thinking back, these qualities about Father Lane quickly come to mind. I remember his gentleness of spirit, his humility and acceptance of poverty and rejection in imitation of his

Master. I think of his devotion and attention to prayer, his deep love and appreciation for the priesthood and his priestly, personal friendship. But he was not in any way timid. Anyone hearing him preach would immediately lose that impression. Whenever occasion presented itself, I would invite him to preach from St. Mary's pulpit. The almost totally white congregation was mesmerized by his uncompromising, straightforward words delivered in a rich, baritone voice. There was no need for a microphone – we all heard him loud and clear. As one parishioner put it, "Simply open all the church windows and all of Gainesville will soon be joining us."

I was placed in Gainesville, Texas, in charge of St. Mary's Parish because the pastor was seriously ill. It proved to be the apex of my priestly duties, and fulfilled me as a priest, a preacher and a pastor. Six months before I left to return to my home diocese in Hamilton, Canada, Sunday Mass attendance was reckoned to be about 90 percent. By that time also, I had been instrumental in forming an ecumenical group involving ministers, local politicians and businessmen. We were beginning to recognize and come to grips with some of the glaring breaches of social justice, especially regarding racial issues and prison reform.

A group of about twenty met weekly for lunch at a prominent local restaurant for purely social reasons. After I had lived in Gainesville for perhaps six months, the men in this group graciously invited me to join them, some of whom I had met casually. I was elated over the prospect, and recognized the potential of this group for improving the social conditions in the neighborhood.

Gradually and gently I began to bring specific problem areas to their attention. Other clergymen were invited to these weekly gatherings. The issues with which we wrestled on those occasions took time and effort in order to develop solutions; but significant progress was being made, to the satisfaction of all involved. Eventually, our group began to realize the importance of our focus and became increasingly eager to discuss and then to take action on ideas. Once we began to understand and accept that every living person on earth was endowed with human dignity by God Himself, we were on our way. We hammered away at this theme week after week! Slowly but surely, we developed a vision of what Gainesville might become.

The pastor of St. Mary's in Gainesville was sick and elderly. Sad to say, he had lost much of his priestly enthusiasm. Upon my arrival he abruptly became available only on occasional Sundays. For the rest of the time he would simply leave town. Within a month, the entire parish operation was left solely in my hands. It was materially and financially in good shape, due to the abundance of oil in the area, but spiritually run down. With mistaken horizontal energy, I set about the task of restoring its fervor.

Earlier I mentioned Father Bill Lane, the pastor of a poor black church in the town. This was in the mid-1950s, prior to the civil rights movement. Father Lane was a most devout priest, and we quickly became fast friends. For a few months he quietly watched my efforts to improve the parish spirit.

The changes I sought were neither evident nor forthcoming. One evening, when he dropped in for dinner, he gently asked me about my own spiritual life. Aware that I was avoiding his questions, he continued to dig away in a most charitable fashion. I know now, God had sent him into my life. The truth gradually surfaced – *nemo dat quod non habet* – you can't give what you haven't got. With tender gracious care, Father Lane stripped away the blindfold and forced me to see for the first time in years how barren was my soul and how ludicrous and worthless my actions.

Truly, God never deserts his priests. We, however, can and do abandon Him. Through his words and especially his example, Father Lane and I began again to make a joint daily Holy Hour, concentrating on the Sacred Humanity of Jesus in the Gospels during these hourly visits.

What a difference it began to make in my recitation of the Rosary. I started to realize that vocal prayer without mental participation is no prayer at all. Gradually, the parish came alive. A Friday night Novena to Our Lady of Perpetual Help attracted ever-increasing numbers of the faithful. There was a heartening increase in the number of parishioners attending daily Mass. The lines outside the confessional became longer. The Legion of

Mary, dormant for many years, was reinvigorated. As a result of its apostolic labor, it brought in many sheep that had been temporarily lost, confused and alienated. Plans were made to start a radio broadcast of Sunday Mass once a month to reach listeners as far away as Dallas.

During this time, a special apostolate was formed at the Gainesville Correctional Center, a local prison, mostly for young women. A group of parishioners began to visit the prison regularly, bringing the consolation of Christ into the lives of the inmates and giving the women a sense of belonging. I began to celebrate Mass in the prison chapel on a regular basis, usually every other week. Initially, I noticed many gaps in the chapel pews. Over time they gradually filled in, and eventually the chapel was full.

The Episcopal Chaplain, Father Joseph Ruth, and I began a cooperative venture to assist these women. Over the years they had developed an acquired taste for lesbianism. To meet this challenge, I devised a plan, shared it with my Episcopalian cohort, Father Joseph Ruth, and he enthusiastically encouraged its implementation.

I traveled to Sherman, Texas, and Ardmore, Oklahoma, to further share my plan with both the Catholic and Protestant chaplains of the Air Force bases located on the outskirts of these cities. I asked them if they would be willing to each send a busload of handpicked young airmen to be present at a social evening in the auditorium of the jail. We arrived at a consensus after I explained why such a novel idea might help these young ladies.

Mrs. Burlingame, the jail superintendent, was the next person whom Father Joseph Ruth and I approached. Initially, she was dubious, but the more we promoted the advantages of the plan, the more comfortable she became with the idea. A date was set, and the first social evening proved to be even better than anticipated. The young men were perfect gentlemen and exhibited exemplary conduct. The incarcerated women proved to be most feminine and charming. One young airman was overheard to say, "Wow! I've never seen so many beautiful women together in one place in my whole life."

The impact of this social event was to turn many of the female inmates away from acquired lesbianism. A number of them began corresponding with the airmen. On occasion a few airmen took time off to visit the women at the jail.

Two years later Mrs. Burlingame remarked that these organized efforts produced great improvement in the lives of many of the women inmates.

This time I had no illusion as to *Who* was the transforming Agent. The simple, honest and very direct St. Teresa of Avila reminds us that true humility is the only cure for pride. Not only does it bring about the destruction of this insidious vice; it further leads to victory over selfishness, greed, blind ambition and lust.

Theologians, are you taking note? Are you paying attention? Are you listening?

My work at the Gainesville Correctional Center taught me two valuable lessons that I hope will never be forgotten. The graces offered by God to his priests are most abundant and, therefore, priests should never take pride in the delusion that they are in command. I am further reminded that there can be no true genuine justice without an outpouring of charity liberally flavored with mercy. The 200 women – mostly young – sentenced to various terms in the facility no doubt were justly detained. That, however, gave no one the right to attempt to take away the dignity and self-respect of the women.

Gradually, as the official Catholic chaplain, my office at the prison became an unofficial place of sanctuary. No matter what internal institutional troubles they encountered, the incarcerated females came to realize that they would always get a fair shake, confidential understanding, an attentive ear and an advocate within the four walls of my office. A further luxury, a carton of Camel cigarettes, could always be found in the lower unlocked, right-hand drawer of my desk for their use. In those days, the carcinogenic effects of cigarette smoke were not well understood. Not a single inmate ever took more than the allotted one or two cigarettes. This service transcended religious denomination lines. Catholic, Protestant, Jew and Gentile – all were made welcome.

An ocean of tears was shed in that office, and there were many angry and frustrated outbursts. Somehow, and I emphasize, with the grace of God, most problems were resolved. As I continued with Father Lane to faithfully make a daily Holy Hour, I came to recognize more and more the face of Jesus in each of the inmates. Time after time the image and the words of the "Good Thief" on Calvary came to mind, "Lord, remember me when you come into your kingdom." And instantly, Jesus replied, "This day you shall be with me in Paradise." (Luke 23:42–43) The thief humbly stole his way into God's celestial kingdom.

A month prior to my permanent departure from Gainesville I was informed that Ann O. wished to see me. I knew of her but had never met her. She was the unofficially recognized leader of the prison subculture. Without a doubt she was one of the most physically attractive young ladies I had ever met. Her visit was dignified, brief and to the point. It surprised me when she apologized for not meeting with me sooner. She informed me that she had received news of my imminent departure from Texas. I deliberately refrained from asking her what grapevine from the outside world had leaked that news to her.

I have never forgotten what she then said; "Thank you for what you have done for all of us who are forced to live here. Most of us trust almost no one, but every woman in this place trusts you, Father Morgan. We are all sorry that you are leaving." I reminded myself again that it was not the hot shot Frank Morgan, but the grace of God given to his priests, that was responsible for whatever good occurred on my watch.

I have many interesting stories of the three years that I spent in Gainesville. When I arrived in town, no provision had been made for my personal transportation. Fortunately, walking was one of my favorite forms of exercise, so it presented no immediate problem. Strolling up and down the streets of the town, I was not likely to miss the homes of many parishioners. Members of the parish were most generous in their offers to drive me. This situation lasted more than a couple of months.

There were several well-to-do parishioners, most of whom were in the oil-production business. One of them, Bernard, asked my help with a complicated marriage problem that entailed considerable correspondence with the Diocesan Marriage Tribunal in Dallas. One hot sunny day, I still recall the temperature – 107 degrees – Bernard and I were scheduled for a meeting at diocesan headquarters. A Tribunal official told us that the problem had been solved in Bernard's favor, and he was now free to marry. I witnessed and blessed the marriage.

As he prepared to leave on his honeymoon, Bernard instructed me to visit a local car dealer who had a message for me. Mystified, I did so. The "message" was a 1952 light green Buick Roadmaster, a gift in appreciation from Bernard. No longer would I have to depend on someone else for a ride!

A couple of years after living in Gainesville I was told the full story of an aging Catholic named Joe, who had led what was termed a "checkered" career. A widower, angry at the world, he lived on a farm with his grown daughter. He had run afoul of the law a few years earlier because of his energetic production of barnyard moonshine. For many years he had run a thriving business, and amassed a considerable fortune through the enthusiastic distribution of the product of his labor.

One day a friend alerted him to an impending raid by the police. Joe promptly gathered his money, sealed it in several airtight jars and hid the jars in strategic locations on his property. He destroyed the apparatus from which he lovingly extracted his homegrown booze. The anticipated raid indeed took place, and the police uncovered sufficient evidence – but not the money – to send him to jail. After serving his sentence, he was a semi-recluse and an aging, embittered man. At no time since his incarceration had he appeared in church.

One of my parishioners told me that he maintained on his farm a large pond well stocked with catfish. With Joe on my mind, I took the matter before our Lord in the Blessed Sacrament. Soon after, I phoned Joe; a friend of his had given me his unlisted number.

"Joe," I began, "this is Father Morgan from St. Mary's."

"Oh, I've heard about you," he responded. "You're that foreigner from Canada with a funny accent."

I let the remark pass. In our conversation I told him of my

fondness for catfish and asked him if I could do a spot of fishing on his property.

There was a long pause. "I thought you were calling because you were after my money," he said.

I corrected him. "I'm only after your catfish and your soul." I was stunned when he broke down and began to cry in great sobbing gasps.

When his grief subsided and his anger was spent, he invited me to his country home, ostensibly to fish. Evidently he was eager to meet me. It's been said that timing is everything. In this case, it proved to be true. Joe was ready to pour out his soul – first to me in conversation and then to God in a genuinely sorrow-filled confession.

The catfish I caught tasted great. His presence at Mass, along with his daughter, every Sunday afterwards, brought great joy to my heart. And his financial contributions to the parish were most generous.

I have warm memories of leading a caravan of cars containing forty Gainesville citizens of varying faiths to the Dallas ice-skating arena. I missed this winter sport while in Texas, and used these excursions to introduce them to this invigorating exercise. Only two or three from this group had ever ice-skated before. I understand that they continued to make these trips long after my departure from their town.

One New Year's Day I was sitting quietly reading in the rectory when the doorbell sounded. A group of seven or eight men from the parish were on their way for a swim in man-made Lake Texoma, a few miles north of town. The temperature was near 80 degrees. The men had made a sudden decision to stop at the rectory to invite me to join them. Such was the camaraderie that had developed during my time among them. I was ready in five minutes. When we arrived at the lake, "the ol' swimmin' hole," there was only one warning: Stay Away From That Clump of Trees. The men warned me that too many copperhead snakes made their homes in that area. Recalling what happened to Adam and Eve, I kept my distance.

During my final Holy Week in Gainesville, Father Lane and I kept busy hearing confessions for several days and many hours, both in his parish church and mine. By 6:00 P.M. on the last day, St. Mary's was finally empty of penitents. I suggested that we have dinner at a local restaurant that I had not previously frequented. He was to be my guest on this occasion. He gratefully accepted. Both of us were tired and famished.

The restaurant was fairly busy as we were shown to our booth. Some fifteen minutes later we were chatting away, and I noticed that groups who arrived after us were being served. No one had even come to take our order. I mentioned it to Father Lane. Yes, he, too, had noticed the lack of service. Stupidly, I failed to understand what was happening. Finally, quietly and patiently, Father Lane said, "Frank, don't you realize why we're not being served?" It hit me like a blow to the stomach – Father Lane was black! I sat there stunned for thirty seconds and then excused myself.

The owner was standing near the cash register. Upon approaching him, he realized he had a very angry, dissatisfied customer on his hands. Almost in a whisper, even though I was seething inside, I asked why the lack of service. Was it my Roman collar that offended him?

He replied with some hesitation, "I have never had a black customer in my restaurant before now."

"Congratulations on finally having one."

Then I lost it completely. I told him that if our orders were not taken in three minutes, I would do two things: First, I would take him outside and would physically thrash him. Yes, I was fully capable of carrying out my threat, even though he was bigger and heavier. Secondly, I told him that on the following Sunday from the pulpit I would ask our parishioners not to patronize his establishment.

He was horrified! He stammered, "But you're a priest. You can't hit me."

"Try me!" I replied.

I returned to our booth. Quite coincidentally the next two groups to come into the restaurant happened to be members of my parish. Noticing us, they came over to our table to say "hello" before being seated and observed that we had not been served. Their expressions of friendliness towards Father Lane were not lost on the restaurant owner. Within thirty seconds a waitress appeared and hurriedly took our order. By the way, we relished the well-prepared meal. Upon departing, the owner came over to us, apologized for his conduct and told us that we were welcome back at any time.

*   *   *   *

Looking back, Gainesville proved to be an important factor in my departure from the Catholic priesthood. It was not my arrival at Gainesville but my departure that devastated me. Without warning, my bishop summoned me home to my Canadian roots. I was crushed! In vain, I attempted to remain and join the Diocese of Dallas. Immediately, I requested permission to seek incardination, an ecclesiastical formality by which I would be transferred from my home diocese in Hamilton to the Dallas diocese. My request was refused.

I packed up my few belongings and sold my 1952 Buick Roadmaster. The money from the sale of the car allowed me to purchase a used Volkswagen Beetle – in the bishop's favorite color: black. I made my somber farewells and headed back to Canada. I was beginning to understand how Moses must have felt when coming down from the top of Mt. Sinai. It was time to return home. As I bade a sorrowful goodbye to this Texas town, I left a good portion of myself.

Gainesville had been my priestly home for three years, a soul-satisfying, memorable time. I developed friendships with several dedicated priests from the nearby towns of Lindsay and Muenster, and life indeed was filled with happiness.

The horizontal habits, I am ashamed to admit, that formerly encrusted me began again to reassert themselves in my priestly activities upon leaving. With dismay I sought permission to be accepted into a missionary society, that of Saint Francis Xavier. I was acquainted with many of its priests due to its proximity to St. Augustine's Seminary. They were stationed both in China and San Salvador. Permission was again refused. I was to remain, under promise of obedience, a priest in my own diocese. My return to Hamilton was in early April. There was still snow on the ground; I promptly caught pneumonia. Within a week I was assigned to a parish as an assistant pastor. Strong feelings persisted that life would never be the same as it had been in Texas. For years I corresponded regularly with a host of my Gainesville friends. To this day, I continue to keep in contact with a family that befriended me during my sojourn there.

A couple of years after departing from Texas, dissatisfaction with my priestly life in Hamilton began nagging me. Wars between vows and friendships, guilt and love raged through my mind. It was so easy to slip into that analytical mind that seemed to be so much a part of my spiritual life at that time. Exorcists, so we are informed, were under no circumstance to engage the devil in conversation. That was a losing battle, a no-win situation. Since Satan continues to maintain his angelic powers, man, unaided, is no match for Lucifer, the bearer of light. How often I had taught and preached about the necessity of prayer in time of temptation, but now my words of wisdom to others went personally unheeded. We are born into this world, not depraved, but with a darkness of understanding, a weakness of will and a strong inclination to evil.

Instead of filling up that place in my heart through personal surrender to God in prayer, I continued to deafen my ears to my own advice and to analyze my temptations with the enthusiastic aid of an imp perched on my shoulder. Today, I wonder how Father Lane dealt with such temptations – surely, they occurred to him. I can see him now, on his knees, alone in his little church, and yet, not alone. There in the tabernacle was his most understanding Friend consoling him. Like Father Lane, this Friend also had known rejection.

Around that time I became aware of a young priest with flaming red hair, from the Resurrectionist teaching order, who had left the active ranks of the priesthood only to return after a few months. My mounting dissatisfaction drove me to visit him.

He was teaching in a high school in a nearby city and was in his mid to late thirties. He was personable, warm and understanding as I shared my frustration with him. Much of my dissatisfaction stemmed from my inability to initiate ways to vitalize the life of the parish where I was assistant pastor. I no longer had the authority to effect changes which I thought would sanctify the faithful and make them more responsive to glaring social needs in the community. He, too, continued to wrestle with thoughts of again departing, this time, permanently, from his priestly duties. Much of his dissatisfaction stemmed from what he described as "living in a glass bowl."

Some of the priests with whom he was associated constantly watched his comings and goings. They monitored his phone messages, his mail and his visitors. It was uncomfortable for him to live under such a cloying cloud of suspicion. His parting advice to me was better to leave sooner than later while employment would be more available due to my age – now approaching forty.

My perplexity was simply this: Was I better off dealing with the devil I knew rather than with the devil I did not know? My struggle continued for four more agonizing years until I finally determined to make my departure. Since my return to Canada, I had lost fifteen pounds, not due to what I was eating, but what was eating me.

*   *   *   *

I had been ordained a priest in 1949. I enjoyed the exhilarating privilege of directing and nurturing the souls in need of spiritual sustenance.

Why had I become a priest?

My truly devout and impoverished Catholic family has to be placed at the top of the list. Added to this influence were the dedicated teaching Sisters of St. Joseph, whom I revere to this day. Most of us never perceived them as cruel or unjust. They expected excellence from us in both conduct and study and taught these qualities, especially by the example of their own lives. Also, there was an overall reverent respect in those days for those in the religious life. Among the many priests I knew at that time, one stands out above all the rest – my uncle, Father Vincent Morgan. He was as "Irish as Paddy's pigs" – a country pastor. In certain ways he was not unlike Barry Fitzgerald who played such a delightful part in *Going My Way*.

In my home diocese of Hamilton, there was no shortage of priestly vocations; in fact, the newly ordained could look forward to twenty-plus years as an assistant before becoming a pastor of a parish in their own right. Our bishop, conscious of the long haul, often took advantage of opportunities to send his younger priests to other needy dioceses and even to mission fields in the Western Hemisphere. Such assignments usually lasted only for a few years. In some limited cases, the clerics, so assigned, sought and were granted permission to remain permanently.

Two years after returning from Texas and in the depths of deep personal discontent, my morale plummeted still further upon learning of the death of my dear good friend, Father Bill Lane. May his gentle soul find eternal rest in the everlasting arms of God!

Gradually, over the ensuing years, the salt again began to lose its savor. Like a lighted candle, I never lost the light of faith; but the zeal, the heat, and the fervor slowly flickered and finally faded. For years I continued to hold on, with little change in my horizontal lifestyle, all the while becoming more vulnerable as Satan assailed me with temptations of hypocrisy. Finally, seemingly unable to go neither up nor down, I determined to go out, to depart, to abandon the priesthood altogether. It was indeed a gut-wrenching day when I said "Good bye" to my bishop.

I made an appointment to see the bishop and together we walked up and down the long driveway outside his residence. We spoke in quiet, deadly serious tones. I reviewed my priestly life with him, the priests with whom I was associated, my falls from grace and, above all, my discouragements. I also reminded him that his first concern must be for the welfare of his priests and recommended a more fatherly approach to their problems. He was inclined, at times, to be overly severe. He listened intently and remarked, "None of my priests have ever spoken so openly to me before and I thank you." I replied, "It's too late for me now, I have burned my bridges through this meeting. Be kind and approachable in the future." With that I knelt on the pavement and asked for his blessing. With tears in his eyes, he begged me to reconsider. However, I had made up my mind and I had crossed my personal Rubicon; I arose and made my departure.

It should be mentioned here that news filtering through from Vatican Council II made my departure easier. Names of expert theologians, *periti*, a collective name by which they were known, took on a familiar ring, familiar in the local secular newspapers. You may recall some of the better known names: Karl Rahner, Hans Küng, Edward Schillebeeckx, Bernard Haering, Charles Davis, Anthony Kosnick, Charles Curran, Richard McCormick and Gregory Baum. These leaders of the band in glowing terms promised a new day of glorious unfiltered living for Roman Catholics. They spoke and wrote of a married priesthood, freedom of individual conscience, the use of artificial birth control, more dialog with all religions, less hierarchical interference, new Bible study without the intrusion of Catholic tradition, less clericalism manifested by priests and nuns by shucking off their religious attire, and open accommodation to the world and its secular influences. Since these progressive theologians were perceived as experts, more and more Catholics bought into their vision, especially as it was repeated over and over again in the secular media, finally filtering into the Catholic religious publications. We never thought at that time to question or examine the lifestyles of these so-called experts.

The pronouncements of these Episcopal consultants only caused me to become more uncomfortable. I suspect, on looking back, I used their pronouncements as further excuses for leaving the priesthood. I told myself over and over that this was not the kind of Church that I had come to know and love. It was many years later that I came to realize that we had been sold a bill of false goods.

How can I describe my life to you up to that time?

Shortly after his death, Archbishop Sheen's autobiography, *Treasure in Clay*, was published. His soaring, inspiring words aptly capture my own sentiments. He wrote:

That autobiography is the crucifix, the inside story of my life, not in the way it walks the stage of time, but how it was recorded, taped and written in the Book of Life. It is not the autobiography that I tell you but the autobiography I read to myself. In the crown of thorns, I see my pride, my grasping for earthly toys in the pierced Hands, my flight from shepherding care in the pierced Feet, my wasted love in the wounded Heart, in my prurient desires of the flesh hanging from Him like purple rags. Almost every time I turn a page of that book, my heart weeps at what eros *has done to* agape, *what the 'I' has done to the 'Thou,' what the professed friend has done to the Beloved.*

For the most part I have shared only passing insights about my immediate family. When I close my eyes and think back, as I often do, even into the 1920s, the thoughts and emotions which surface are those of self-sacrificing devotion, warmth, concern for the five children, poverty and hard work, particularly at the beginning of the Great Depression, great family communication, especially at the dinner hour, assigned family chores, the importance of education and study, deep love and respect for the church and its clergy.

When I stop to listen closely, I can hear Mother singing her favorite hymns as she went about preparing meals in the kitchen. My three sisters, scurrying around, would join in with her. My brother and I would be busy at our books or carrying out the chores assigned to us; the ever present weeds, especially dandelions in the garden, taking out the garbage, sifting the ashes from the furnace to retrieve chunks of unburned coal, cleaning the floors, shoveling snow.

Like so many women, Mother had great intuition. She could spot a phony a mile away and had no hidden agenda when speaking her mind. I suspect she was prepared to dislike Ruth before they met. She admitted to me afterwards how much she was impressed with my wife and how quickly they took to each other right from the beginning. Mother was also the chief family disciplinarian. Only if an issue became serious would she refer it to Dad, usually after the completion of the evening meal. Taking the person, or persons, aside, a few well-spoken words from him, quietly but firmly, usually put us back on course. The formula for my parents' success in raising us was simple – they led and taught by example.

When Mother died, I recall writing to my brother, Vincent, then a Jesuit priest working in the foothills of the Himalayan Mountains in India. In the letter I stated, "If there was anything about Mother I might wish to have been different, I can't imagine what it might be."

Dad and I were very close, I have always thought, although there were no favorites. We were all loved dearly and equally. He left school to go to work after completing only four years of formal education. However, he loved to read with intense concentration and through the years studied world history, geography, politics, theology. Everything was grist for the mill. Communication around the dinner table was especially animated, filled with laughter and often instructional – usually initiated by a comment or question from dad. He was a teller of tall tales, stories from his past, singer of humorous songs, a buck-and-wing dancer, and carpenter. Our playhouse and swing that he built in the backyard were magnets for the children in the neighborhood.

Dad also loved to write poetry. Like Mother, he was born in Collingwood, Ontario. On the occasion of that town's centennial celebration, he submitted a poem of reminiscences to the *Collingwood Enterprise Bulletin*, the town's only newspaper. What a delightful surprise he received when his contribution was printed on the front page of the centennial edition, front and center from the top of the page to the bottom. Not bad for four years of formal education!

It's no wonder I continue to grieve over the pain I caused these two beautiful people, as well as to my brother and sisters. Never a day goes by without a large ache in my heart. As I write these words, tears fill my eyes and obscure my vision. How often I yearn to put my arms around Mom and Dad to tell them of the deep sorrow in my heart for the sorrow I caused them and to ask their forgiveness.

I have never been able to honestly justify my departure from the priesthood. The rejections that have come into my life as a result, I have tried to accept as a matter of simple justice for my self-centeredness. God does not send these hurtful occasions in any punitive sense! Rather, I perceive them as salutary reminders of my need to repair the damage that was caused by my sins and selfish behavior in turning my back on my first love.

SIX

Factory Worker Priests
and Family Ties

The righteousness of the upright delivers them,
but the unfaithful are trapped by evil desires.
     Proverbs 11:6

Two years prior to my leaving the priesthood, as I more and more considered its real possibility, I began to be beset with a multitude of conflicting emotional upheavals attempting to tear me apart. Feelings of failure, betrayal, guilt, hypocrisy, scandal, shame, indecisiveness and the pain that my leaving would cause to my family and friends resulted in severe inner turmoil. I attempted to justify my thoughts of leaving by looking outside myself for the causes of my problems.

I mistakenly perceived that my clerical friends had deliberately deserted me. I rarely met with them anymore. There was a small group of priests in the neighborhood who met regularly. Due to my preoccupation with an alcoholic priest in our rectory, they never invited our participation. Loneliness began to set in, a feeling I had rarely felt before. Since there were few priests with whom to associate, I sought company and solace among the parishioners. This only added fuel to the fire since I sought them for the wrong reasons – not to assist and serve them but to solicit and accept support from them. It solved nothing.

I needed something different in my priestly activities, something to recapture my fervor. All this time it was right there before my nose – turning in prayer to my heavenly Father for assistance – but no – I was slowly but surely becoming blind to both my sickness and its cure. How often I had preached about the meaning of the opening words of *The Lord's Prayer*, "Our Father who art in heaven." The words simply mean placing our total trust in God since our heavenly Father constantly cares for His children. If only I had turned to Him in fervent, beseeching prayer! What a blindfold I was weaving for myself.

Suddenly, the solution came to me (or so I thought). It was the custom for parish priests to present individual religious instructions to those interested in investigating the doctrines and practices of the Catholic faith. These sessions took hours of time each week, mostly during the evening hours from 7:00 P.M. until sometimes 10:00 P.M.

A group of Paulist priests in Toronto had started giving group instructions to those interested, advertising in the daily press. I took time one afternoon to make the hour's drive to their headquarters to become acquainted with their format. They were most informative, cooperative and gratified with my interest. However, the pastor of the parish in which they labored warned me not to expect too much from the classes – in a class of fifteen or twenty, I should expect no more than perhaps five converts to the Catholic faith.

Forewarned and forearmed, I immediately set about developing the details. Desiring to make the encounters warm and homey, I checked the rectory basement searching for adequate quarters. Not very promising but perhaps adequate, I decided. It was an unfinished basement, dirty and dusty. Keep in mind, I was desperate to do battle with my inner conflicts and accordingly set about cleaning a room with a vengeance. I labored for a good week to make it at least half presentable. A table, chairs, even a record player for soft music before class, plus the acquisition of a screen for filmstrip presentations were strategically placed in our little rustic quarters.

When all was in readiness, I began an advertising campaign, not citywide, but on a more modest scale through the use of our own and neighboring parish Sunday bulletins. The results were gratifying with, I recall, twenty-one affirmative replies. We began our first class in September and continued weekly for twenty weeks. Would we get at least five converts? No, instead, there were seventeen who asked to be received into the church. I felt a surge of hope welling up within me.

The pastor was delighted and arranged for a parish ceremony to celebrate the entrance of these new parishioners into our ranks. In fact, he became so enthusiastic and involved that he decided to totally take over the ceremony himself. As he welcomed them into their new spiritual home, I sat on the sidelines in the sanctuary as a spectator. Happy for the new members but also dejected, disappointed and disillusioned! The old devil "pride" was beginning to reassert itself in my soul. I was soon back at square one where I had parked my emotional demons that quickly returned to haunt me.

During the week immediately before my leaving the active priesthood, I was suddenly overcome with fear that I was losing my mind. I hurried to Toronto and visited a Jesuit priest friend whom I had met through my brother, Vincent, who is also a Jesuit. Father J., I'll call him. He had a doctorate in psychology and was a most gentle person. I poured out my concerns to him and asked him to check out my sanity. I owe him a large debt of gratitude. Not only did he offer me room and board for the next three days; he threw every psychological test in his arsenal at me. He immersed me in paperwork that, curiously, I enjoyed and gobbled up one test after another.

Two days following the tests, Father J. presented me with his complete findings. No, I was not crazy; I was not demented; I was not out of my mind. I had strong social concerns but was confused over values.

The tests revealed that I had told the truth about myself in every instance. There was one especially significant fact that I have never forgotten. He warned me most seriously that if I did not pursue a regular regimen of serious study, depression, in all likelihood, would result. This was noted in the intelligence test. I still recall that there were sixty problems to solve in the test – each succeeding one more difficult. In our post-test meeting I informed him that I was certain I had correctly solved fifty-nine of these problems. I then told him further that the last problem, the sixtieth, contained no solution, i.e., that it was insoluble. I can still see him laughing as he informed me that I had received the highest mark of anyone he had ever tested.

Since that day, driven by that dire warning, I have tried to keep on the cutting edge of theology. I may be the only inactive priest today who is a member of the Fellowship of Catholic Scholars founded by the great and beloved Monsignor George Kelly, now deceased. What a wonderful support group it has proven to be, consistently supporting Roman Catholic practice and loyalty! Its quarterly publications are scholarly, thoroughly orthodox, stimulating and thought provoking. Its bylaws totally parallel my thinking and sentiments on both pre- and post-Vatican Council II. The fellowship now comprises several hundred members; made up of bishops, priests, university professors and college-educated laypersons.

Clergy or laity, each of us needs the support of others; someone who is close enough to us to be able to mirror back our image, echo back our words so that we can see how we appear and sound to the world outside us.

*   *   *   *

As I prepared to leave the active priesthood I met with the pastor to inform him of my decision. I still remember to this day the haunted expression on his face. In the early morning hours as I slowly backed out of the rectory driveway, I said goodbye to him as he pleaded with me to stay. It was an overcast day but not nearly as gloomy as the darkness that had settled around my heart. A thousand times I panicked as I drove westward. A thousand times the urge assailed me to turn around and head back to my parish home. But ideas, both good and bad, have consequences as I figuratively journeyed downward from Jerusalem to Jericho. I must bite the bullet; there was no turning back.

The month was May of 1964. Suddenly I was on my own. I can never fully express the agony I felt, especially during that first month of my departure. I envisioned myself as another Judas. Nightly I would awaken in the darkness surrounding me, my complete being immersed in terror, loneliness and despair that seemed to bring me to the brink of hell itself. This gut-wrenching time in my life, never to be forgotten, subsided only gradually.

I had put aside sufficient money to rent a small, furnished apartment in a city many miles away. Now, to obtain gainful employment . . .

My first job was selling for Fuller Brush. This well-known company employed thousands of sales people in the 1960s selling home cleaning equipment door-to-door. On the first day, I went out full of confidence. It was the wake-up call I really needed. As Father Morgan, I was made welcome in every home I visited in any parish. Now, doors were firmly closed with comments such as, "Sorry, not interested" or "I'm too busy to stand here listening to you" or "Perhaps some other time but not today." So, Father Morgan was not the hot shot he thought he was. It was great for his humility but not for his pocketbook. That job lasted for a record short time.

A job notice appeared in the local newspaper and caught my attention. It was for the position of assistant personnel director at the Wolverine Tube Company. This was a fair-sized, unionized company that manufactured all sorts of tubing for a variety of operations. I applied for the job and was elated to learn that I had been selected for the position. In completing the company application I stated that I had recently left the priesthood since I saw no sense in covering up my past.

After I began work, the personnel director told me that he planned to leave his position within the year and would concentrate on grooming me for his vacated slot. Further, I learned that the union planned to go on strike unless the employees' demands for better wages and benefits were met. The deadline was three months away. I had arrived, so I naively thought.

The company nurse at Wolverine was Catholic. Upon reading my employment application she was horrified to learn that I was a "spoiled" priest! That very evening she made it a point to set up an emergency meeting with the pastor of the local parish. His advice to her was instant and direct. "Make trouble for Frank. Do everything in your power to get him out of there." Their concern was the scandal that my presence in the area would cause.

On the following morning, she informed the personnel director of her plans based on the advice she had received from her pastor. The director took me into his private office to share this information with me. Then he stood up, asked me to stay on and assured me that he would fight to keep me as his assistant.

In his eyes nothing had changed. My conscience, still attempting to adjust to this unfamiliar secular environment, urged otherwise. Reluctantly and with a heavy heart, I departed from this most promising position to search elsewhere for employment. Over many years I had tried to learn the hard lesson that when I forgive, I really free myself from the bitter ties that bind me to the one who hurts me. I must, however, confess that I have not always been successful in my efforts. My will said "Yes," but my emotions indicated an unequivocal "No!"

For two months during the summer of 1964, I accepted a temporary position with a Children's Aid Society, which I used as a time of personal adjustment. The work itself proved less than gratifying with its mountain of paperwork. It reminded me of the three greatest lies told in the history of the world. One: Your check is in the mail. Two: I'll still respect you in the morning. Three: I'm from the government and I am here to help you.

Since necessity is the mother of invention, I developed a certain skill in searching for positions. An ad in the local unemployment office caught my eye. A position was offered for a psychiatric rehabilitation officer in the Ontario Department of Health. Evidently, I had developed decent job interview skills and was welcomed into that position. The director of the office was a young, energetic, knowledgeable man in his early forties named Alex O'Neill. Born in Ireland, he quickly instructed me on the job requirements, introduced me into the prevailing Irish culture and into a much-needed social life. Alex also had a hands-on familiarity with every Irish pub and social club in the city, or so it seemed.

It was one of the more pleasant experiences I had since leaving the priesthood. Suddenly, I had friends, plus helpful, understanding working partners. The work itself was varied, challenging and creative.

Within a year I was promoted to the position of director of

psychiatric rehabilitation services for Western Ontario, head-quartered in Windsor. Alex O'Neill was delighted. In this way we would continue to work together but now on an equal basis.

Moving to Windsor in 1965 caused no problem since I had few possessions. Serendipitously, living quarters, plus meals, were available to me at minimum cost in the physicians' residence quarters of the psychiatric hospital. Dr. Jim Bryce, the director of the unit, and I became good friends. We would spend hours in the evening discussing problems about our patients – each supporting one another. Again, the work was demanding, challenging and rewarding as we tried to alleviate the problems of some of God's most misunderstood children. I attended Mass on Sundays but maintained an arm's-length association with the priests in the area, since my level of trust in clergy support was at low tide.

During this period, which was two years after I had left the priesthood, I met my future wife, Ruth-Ellen, who was visiting mutual friends on their wedding anniversary. As she descended the steps from the airplane, I was immediately attracted to her. She was petite, red-haired and slightly freckled-faced: all external signs of an impish personality. She bore a distinct resemblance to Susan Hayward, the movie actress of the 1950s.

As we drove with our friends to their home, I found it surprisingly easy to converse with her. She was quick, bright and definitely had a mind of her own. Our conversation ended in the wee hours of the morning. With a sense of, shall I say, panic, I suddenly realized that I had been mesmerized by this elfin female and was hooked – line and sinker.

As we got to know each other, the attraction to married life became more appealing. I began to have vivid recollections of the wonderful families I had so often visited as a priest. For example, often on a Saturday evening following confessions in Kitchener, I would walk to the home of Walter and Mary Rich. As their four children got ready for bed, we would sit in their kitchen eating bowls of cereal. Walter would tease Mary unmercifully. I can still hear Mary's soft laughter in return. They remain in my memory as a model loving couple. Sometimes, as I returned to the rectory, it was with a touch of longing for such marital bliss. I would quickly say a prayer and put the thought out of my mind.

Ruth had received instruction in the Catholic faith while in her early 20s, living and working outside of Montreal, Quebec. Upon completion of the religious course, she was asked to sign a document issued by the Diocese of Montreal regarding her consent to become a Catholic. She was appalled to read the opening statement: "I, Ruth-Ellen, being a pagan . . . " Pagan? She was anything but; she was active in her own faith by regularly attending Sunday services and participating enthusiastically in the activities of her faith community. Her interest in becoming a Catholic quickly dwindled because of such arrogant insensitivity. Just prior to our marriage, she showed me the document; she had kept it in her Bible. In my anger I ripped it to shreds. It would be many years before she would again consider joining the Catholic faith. Through the grace of God, this eventual change of heart took the influence of a great Catholic layman and an outstanding priest.

Since my working situation had significantly improved, marriage became a reality. In October of 1966, nine months after we had met, Ruth and I were married in a quiet civil ceremony. Later, we had our marriage validated by a social activist priest in Detroit, Father Maurice Geary.

My rehabilitation experiences brought me into contact with companies in the Detroit area and led to another employment offer as a counselor with Goodwill Industries. Ruth and I packed up our worldly possessions and, in November 1966, armed with all necessary official government papers, we moved to Troy, Michigan. Since then, the United States has been our permanent home.

Shortly thereafter, the State of Michigan funded a program through Goodwill to train severely mentally disabled adults. I was offered the position of manager for the operation, and readily accepted it.

When living in Troy, a northern Detroit suburb, Ruth became executive secretary to the Reverend Harold DeWindt, Presbyterian minister at Kirk-in-the-Hills. Situated on a low hill above a beautiful inland lake in Bloomfield Hills, it is regarded by many as the most impressive church structure in all of Michigan. People came from far and wide to admire the magnificent Gothic church, with its beautiful manicured lawn sloping gently to the banks of a crystal clear lake.

The congregation was also drawn to its pastor's inspirational preaching and enraptured by its professional choir. Reverend DeWindt did everything possible to encourage me to join the ranks of the Presbyterian clergy. He even offered to fund my course of studies. I kindly but firmly refused his offer because of the respect I had never lost for the dignity of the Catholic priesthood. However, his generosity and kindness remains with me today. I couldn't help but compare it to the way in which I had been rejected and opposed by my over-zealous misguided brother priests.

One quiet Sunday afternoon, the phone rang. It was the pastor from my home parish, calling to tell me that my eighty-three-year-old father had died. It was the first of two momentous events in my life in that year of 1967. As if the news of my dad's death were not tragic enough, he instructed me in no uncertain terms **not to attend the Funeral Mass** and to visit the funeral home only after dark or early in the morning and when only the funeral director was present. Furthermore, since our family home was directly across from the rectory and church, I was instructed by the parish priest to park my car, which had American license plates, on a side street, away from the public gaze in order to safeguard the sensibilities of any parishioners in the neighborhood who might be passing by. This, of course, was overkill, purely punitive, not salutary!

When the abrupt phone call was completed, I felt I had been torn apart. Overwhelmed with grief, I wept for the sorrow I had caused my loving dad. How good he had been to me! What a loving father he had been to all of his children. Afterwards, feelings of rage filled my inner being toward this pastor meting out his draconian form of justice with a total lack of mercy.

When my grief and anger subsided, I began to put my thinking into perspective. I did not wish my presence to be a cause of disruption at this sorrowful time for my family. I had already caused them sufficient grief by leaving the active priesthood. In

spite of the fact that in a brief three minutes I had received a
sword in my heart and a knife in my back, I reluctantly determined to obey the pastor's injunctions. It was only after many
years and much prayer that I could forgive his harsh treatment.

It was different for Ruth. Over time she experienced the suffering I endured and resented the callous disregard on the part
of priests toward me – like a mother cub watching over her family. The clerical lack of concern for a brotherly priest in mourn-
ing filled her with disgust. She could not fathom how one priest
could treat another priest, even though fallen, with such lack of
Christian charity.

My mother afterwards asked me to promise that when she
died, Ruth and I would be publicly and prominently present at
both the funeral home and at the Mass of Christian Burial. It was
a promise lovingly carried out ten years later, and it also allowed
me the joy of embracing many old and dear friends once again.
Mother, too, died at age eighty-three, some ten years after my
father, when the stigma of my leaving the active priesthood had
greatly diminished.

I could not have wished for better or more loving parents.
With my one brother and three sisters, we were a close-knit family. The Great Depression that had devastated the United States
was felt as severely in Canada. Dad, a faithful employee of
Canadian Westinghouse, was laid off. Both he and Mother had
to scurry around to make ends meet to support their five young
children. Through his contacts, Dad developed a fledgling enterprise in the sale of beer and liquor. It grew into a flourishing
business. He continued to run it, even after economic conditions
improved and he returned to the Westinghouse plant.

As a devout Catholic, in thanksgiving, he became one of the
chief contributors to our parish, even though not among the
wealthiest.

My brother, Vincent, had entered the Jesuits a couple of years
before I entered the seminary. He became known as an ideal
member of the Society of Jesus – one of God's iron men, completely devoted to the Jesuit constitution and to the Holy Father.
A couple of years before ordination he was assigned to
Darjeeling, India, in the foothills of the Himalayas. There he

spent the next forty-five years teaching at St. Joseph's College and preaching retreats on the *Spiritual Exercises of St. Ignatius of Loyola*, the founder of the Jesuits.

It was during a retreat in Darjeeling where Mother Teresa, who was born in Albania, received the call to begin her great missionary apostolate in Calcutta. This great missionary work rapidly spread to many countries throughout the world. Her method was simple and direct – pray as if everything depended on God, work as if everything depended on you.

I recall asking my brother if he knew Mother Teresa in Darjeeling. He replied, "Yes," and added how approachable and down to earth she was. I then asked him if he were involved in the retreat she had made. He only smiled and changed the subject. He is such a humble, holy priest that I can only surmise.

Vincent, now in his mid eighties, is back in Canada as Spiritual Director to the Carmelite sisters at their convent in Mississauga, Ontario, and chaplain to their nursing home. He leaves the premises infrequently, except for his usual daily walk. In winter, he further exercises by shoveling snow from the nursing home pathways. Whenever we visit my family in Hamilton, I always make it a point to spend time with him. Recently, when I was driving him around to visit our haunts of yesteryear, I remarked that I would like to die with my boots on. He expressed delight and responded, "That's my wish, too."

From the time we started attending St. Anne's Grade School, we went to daily Mass at 7:15 A.M. All five children and Mother were present while Dad started off to work. Vincent and I entered the church by the left-side door, mother and my three sisters by the right-side door. Even as a young boy, Vincent manifested great discipline and devotion. All in the family were quite certain he would one day become a priest. Years after his ordination which took place in India, a Jesuit priest, who knew my brother well, informed me that among the ranks of the Jesuits, who were known for their discipline, he was recognized as a student and later as a priest with an uncompromising will – a man among men.

How much we need a return of those great Jesuit iron men – minds filled with steel and wills filled with zeal – and yet with an over-riding gentle spirit of love.

My middle sister, Agnes, entered the Convent of St. Joseph in Hamilton, where she studied to become a teacher and a dedicated school principal. Following Vatican II, the handwriting was on the wall. The sisters stopped wearing their religious habits. Many gave up community life in favor of apartment living. Social activism took precedence over meditation, Mass and prayer. Exasperated after her many years of dedicated service, Agnes gave up her convent life with sorrow and regret.

Today, Agnes meets weekly with sisters and faithful parishioners in her home. They read and study authentic Catholic doctrine and practices as an antidote to rampant secular humanism.

My three sisters continue to attend Mass daily. Margaret, the eldest, and Rita, the youngest, both lost their husbands before they were thirty years old and both have since remarried. They all live on the same street, and it is a happy occasion when we visit with them reminiscing about old friends, many of whom have now passed into eternity. I daily thank God for the robust health with which God has blessed my brother, my three sisters and me.

I mentioned having two monumental events in my life in 1967. The second one was that Ruth became pregnant with our first-born, David.

SEVEN

One Hundred and Twenty Contacts and Counting

Come to me, all you who are weary and burdened and I will give you rest.
Matthew 11:28

The decision to leave the priesthood is more profound than the decision to enter it. We know today that thousands of priests have left the Catholic Church in the past four decades. But prior to that time, in the era of my ordination, it was a rare phenomenon rarely publicized; so rare – at least in my experience – I wondered if I might be the only priest in Christendom inflicted with this soul-wrenching torment. My rational self told me that there had to be some kindred souls out there. My questions were: Where were they? What were they doing? How were they managing? Could I help them? Could they help me? Could I learn from them?

Three years later, when I had achieved a certain degree of peace with my non-clerical lifestyle, and had settled down to the privileges and responsibilities of married life with Ruth in Troy, Michigan, these questions continued to nag me. It hadn't been easy for me to land the right job, and I empathized deeply with inactive priests, as I prefer to call us, with education and experience of pathetically less liquidity in the marketplace of civilian employment. I, however, finally now had a steady job, and I felt a great need to help my colleagues negotiate their desperately straitened economic and emotional circumstances with an infusion of my new knowledge and experience. But to help them, I first had to find them. I pondered long and hard over whom might be interested in working with me in this area, and where I could obtain guidance.

I happened to be on the University of Detroit campus one spring day in 1967, inquiring about furthering my own education, when I met someone who I felt God had delivered to work with me in this endeavor. In the Jesuit residence building I was introduced to the Vice President of the University, Father James McGlynn. He was middle-aged, vibrant and compassionate. From our first meeting I had a strong premonition that at last the support for which I had searched so long from among my priestly confreres had been found.

The following weekend we talked about the possible plight of priests who had left the active priesthood, especially in recent years. I had organized my concerns into four specific channels: Do some of them need employment? Do any seek reconciliation with the Church? Do they perhaps require an enhanced social life to include an association with other such inactive priests as well as with dedicated active priests? Do they need educational upgrading to better adjust to their activities in the secular world?

Father McGlynn listened, sat back and closed his eyes while pondering these possibilities. Finally, he said, "Frank, for our plan to work (I was delighted to hear his use of that word 'our') you will have to go public with your leaving the ranks of the priesthood." He warned me that I ran the danger of receiving flak for taking a public stance, but he promised to defend my actions to the hilt.

How refreshing it was to speak to such a courageous priest!

We chose *Contact* as the name of our proposed organization. Father McGlynn was a man of action. Within forty-eight hours arrangements were made for me to be interviewed by both the *Detroit News* and *Detroit Free Press*. The stories specified my home telephone number as a point of contact.

The first response from the articles came the very next morning from Joe, a soft-spoken, thoughtful, bearded man who had left the order of the Holy Ghost Fathers a couple of years previously. He was a professor at a suburban college, teaching philosophy and ethics. His classes were fully attended, with a waiting list of interested students.

What was the secret of his classroom popularity? He told me that he had developed the course straight out of the writings of St. Thomas Aquinas, but kept this fact to himself lest it blow his cover as a priest. Faculty and students alike were fascinated by the substance and well ordered reasoning of Joe's lectures. He held this teaching post for many years, revered by fellow professors for his intellectual gifts, gentleness and kindness.

Joe was materially secure and comfortable, and I wondered what had triggered his telephone call. I discovered that he craved the association of like-minded priests who could understand his thinking and respond to his problems. Very few, if any, of his college associates were aware of his background.

I still remember his first visit with Ruth and me. He brought his wife, Laura, and baby son, Joseph, Jr. It was the start of a long friendship. Over time, the haunted, fearful look in his eyes gradually waned. Months later he told me of the comfort and freedom he felt within himself. A great weight had been lifted from him and his troubled sleep had been replaced with peaceful rest at night. It was then that I really understood that immortal line from *Macbeth*: "Sleep that knits up the raveled sleeve of care."

Our home telephone began jangling repeatedly. Connecticut-born Gabe, another religious order priest, was then living in inner city Detroit with his wife, Marian, infant son, Joseph, and his mother-in-law. He had been living in the city during the horrendous civil disturbances in the summer of 1967, when their black neighbors spirited them out of the area because there was a liquor store on the corner of their street that had been looted. While they were temporarily cared for in white suburbia by a dedicated Catholic couple, their black inner city neighbors watched over their home and meager possessions until peace reigned again in the city.

Gabe was working at that time in an entry-level job and was in dire need of decent employment. Through Father McGlynn, he began a training program that paved the way for a promising career in rehabilitation counseling.

Shortly afterwards Gabe and Marian, who had been a religious sister, arrived on our doorstep with another couple. Gub (a nickname) was also an inactive priest, although at that time this term was not current; and Mary, his wife, was also a former religious sister. Now we had Gabe and Gub, Marian and Mary, as new found friends.

A young Jesuit rang our doorbell at 2:00 A.M. one weekday morning. He was a tall, handsome priest attired in clerical garb – black suit and Roman collar. I have rarely seen such a troubled, sorrowful expression. He had recently left the Society of Jesus, and his conscience was causing him great agony. My first attempt was to encourage him to return to his order, but he had already made the decision to leave. There was no difficulty in obtaining a position for him; he had a doctorate degree. Consequently, a large auto company was delighted to obtain his services in its administrative sector.

Telephone calls kept coming into Contact regularly. It was gratifying to hear words of encouragement and offers of assistance from priests who were active in their ministries. Surprisingly, at no time did we receive any condemnatory calls. We did, however, receive only one anonymous letter castigating me with hellfire and brimstone for my evil action of leaving the priesthood.

My own conscience has upbraided me similarly over the years. However, this in no way implicates my relationship with Ruth whom I met two years after I left the active clerical ranks.

During this busy period, when Contact was a still a fledgling, I received a telephone call from the Chancery Office of the Archdiocese of Detroit. It was a message from the priest-spokesman for John Cardinal Dearden, affectionately referred to as Iron John by those close to him – only among themselves, *never* to his face. I wondered if the call contained a message that he was about to close down what we had hardly begun. By no means! The Cardinal asked if I would consent to be interviewed on a radio program entitled *Focus*, moderated by WJR's hugely popular Irishman, J.P. McCarthy.

I was stunned but recovered in time to ask, "Why?" The priest-spokesman informed me that J.P. had recently interviewed an ex-priest (again, there is no such animal – once a priest, always a priest. You can take the man away from the priesthood but you can't take the priesthood away from the man). The inactive priest in question, Father Longo, had written a book of falsehoods and unwarranted condemnations on the Catholic Church. When I called J.P.'s secretary to arrange the interview, I learned that WJR had been deluged with criticism following Father Longo's radio session. J.P. was eager to repair the damage.

J.P. interviewed me in late summer of 1967. More than once during the half-hour session, I had the strangest feeling – here I was, a defector from the most sublime vocation imaginable, defending the Catholic Church and its priesthood! From my standpoint the interview went very well; it allowed me to place Fr. Longo's views into perspective. WJR's ratings must have experienced a substantial boost because the station called to arrange another interview for the following Sunday night, this time with its highly popular host, Hal Youngblood.

From the outset, Father McGlynn and I had determined that Contact would be used *only in support of – and in obedience to – the Church*. It would never be used to encourage priests to leave their vocation. Its purpose was not only to help those who had already left the active ranks but also to encourage and assist in every way possible those who might be tempted to leave, to stay the course. To be sure, many among us hoped that the Vatican might smile favorably on a married priesthood. This was especially so after the close of Vatican II, when changes abounded and moorings had been cast aside. However, the rules following the official decrees of the Church were observed to the letter.

In the autumn of 1967, with Contact less than a few months off the ground, the phone really began to ring in earnest! In response to this burgeoning interest, we began a series of regular meetings at the University of Detroit. These drew an average attendance of forty or more. The greatest number comprised inactive priests but included active clerics and interested laypersons. Every now and then an auxiliary bishop or two would lend his episcopal presence.[1]

1   Three future Michigan bishops - Thomas Gumbleton, Kenneth Untener and Patrick Cooney - were sometimes present at our monthly meetings.

These early meetings soon translated into a process to provide our needy priests with limited financial support and a process to equip them with the proper training and education leading to employment. The University of Detroit offered them undergraduate and graduate courses at reduced rates.

For those requesting laicization (for lack of a better word) the auxiliary bishops who had come to the meetings set up the necessary mechanisms at the Chancery Office in Detroit which forwarded the requests to Rome.

Laicization is a term that has been coined to indicate the reduction of a Roman Catholic priest to the lay state. Since the priesthood, like the Sacrament of Baptism, leaves an indelible mark on the soul, the priesthood remains forever. However, a priest who has left the active ministry can petition Rome through his bishop or superior to have his priestly faculties suspended and his priestly responsibilities removed. The Church removes the celibacy obligation from him and he is permitted to marry within the Church. However, he is not allowed to celebrate Mass or to hear Confessions except under most extraordinary circumstances – at the point of death.

When no other priest is available, an inactive priest is permitted to hear that person's Confession. It has happened to me on two occasions and I thank God that He made me available to assist these two dying souls.

The first such confession was occasioned by a serious auto accident I noticed while driving one dark night. The flashing lights of the ambulance attracted me to stop. Lying on the shoulder of the road was a young man, barely conscious, apparently at the brink of death. I quickly knelt down, put face close to his and informed him that I was a priest. I detected a peaceful smile forming and can still remember his words: "Thank God for

So, too, was the well-beloved Bishop Joseph Schoehner, who baptized our second-born son, Patrick, at the magnificent cathedral on Woodward Avenue in Detroit. Mark and Lynn Vaughn were the godparents for Patrick. Father James McGlynn baptized our first-born, David, at The Gesu Parish in Detroit with Ann and Gerald Fisher as godparents. This dear couple, parents to four young children, had early on taken us to their hearts and home.

sending a priest to me. Father, I am not a fighter, I'm a lover." I prepared him for his Confession and then pronounced those beautiful and consoling words of absolution over him. He passed into unconsciousness and I remained until the ambulance was ready to leave, requesting the driver to contact the hospital Catholic Chaplain.

The second time God granted me the privilege to exercise this priestly sacramental function began with a rather vitally concerned telephone call from a devoted and devout wife whose husband was dying from cancer. She felt he was about to expire and was unable to locate her parish priest. Since she was aware of my clerical background, she requested my assistance. In short order, I arrived at their home in our town. Observing the countenance of the seriously ill husband, whom I had visited from time to time, I realized he was *"in articulo mortis"* (at the point of death). Quickly, I prepared him for Confession and administered absolution. Shortly thereafter, he was in the merciful hands of God. I thank our heavenly Father for these inestimable blessings granted to me.

*   *   *   *

To return to the narrative portion, by this time Contact had expanded to include a broad array of concerned Catholic laypersons. Psychologists offering their professional services counseled that an active social life was vital to the emotional wellbeing of priests recently departed from the active priesthood. Otherwise they tended to be miserable loners, isolated in depressed financial and emotional circumstances, vacillating guiltily over their decision to opt out, anxious to avoid all human contact. To counter this lethal drift, Contact embarked on a purposeful program of social events including parties, dances and mixers. For those hungry for a social life among priestly sympathetic friends, it was there for the asking.

In the midst of all this activity we received a sizeable donation from a prominent bishop in a western diocese. Attached was a beautifully encouraging letter. A year or so later, it was reported that this same bishop had left his diocese to marry.

Joining Father McGlynn in the administration of Contact

was Doctor Robert O'Neill, the personable head of the University of Detroit psychology department, who had his own head on straight. African-born Irish Catholic Hugh McCann, a reporter at the *Detroit Free Press* and later a science reporter at the *Detroit News*, lent his considerable common sense, wit, talents and practical skills to our group. All three men made themselves available to assist in healing many men who carried deep emotional scars.

During approximately four years, Father McGlynn kept a record of all who passed through our hands. He counted 120 inactive priests we had come to know and help. Over the years I have maintained contact with only a few of these men; some have passed totally out of our lives and moved to other parts of the country and even to foreign soils. All I look forward to meeting again – God willing.

With things going so well generally for Contact, it was only human to expect our good fortune to continue. But common sense warned us always to be ready for a change in the weather.

Word came to me from an inactive priest from Windsor, Ontario, just across the border from Detroit, that the resident bishop from the London, Ontario diocese had addressed a parish group in Windsor. The bishop used this occasion for a frontal attack on Contact, describing it as a dissident group of disgruntled ex-priests – traitors to the faith. A letter, signed by Father McGlynn, Doctor Robert O'Neill and me, was quickly dispatched to him in London. It explained the objectives of Contact and included an invitation to meet with us in Windsor.

We never received a response. This, unfortunately, has become a common tactic among many dissenters today – and not a few bishops. The cowardly, demeaning practice of hit-run-and-hide only results in harm and never in healing, correction or understanding. Manliness is a characteristic that needs to be easily recognized in all priests – and bishops.

A nagging concern that repeatedly came to mind centered itself on more efficient ways of obtaining employment for some of the inactive priests who were mired in jobs with little opportunity for upward mobility. One day I took time to visit a headhunter (employment counselor). I patiently told him about my background and what Contact was attempting to achieve. I recall that he, himself, was not a Catholic. Initially, he hesitated, feeling uncomfortable and openly wondered if this visit might be a total waste of his time. It was then that a light went on in my head (an inspiration from the Holy Spirit?) and I said to him, "Why not use me as your guinea pig?"

Apparently, that got his attention.

He was a big fellow who looked me up and down and said, "Quite frankly, you are not the kind of promising prospect I look for to place in an available position. You're not very big, your work history is extremely limited and you are already in your forties."

I persisted, "Why not try me right now! Is there a decent job you currently have available?"

He told me of one promising position, adding that my chances were slim to none in being hired. It involved an emerging department in Michigan Blue Cross/Blue Shield whose purpose was to monitor newly developed Medicare guidelines. With some reluctance he set up an interview for the following day.

The interview was a lengthy one involving a series of tests that I ably completed. I was then questioned by a psychologist and two physicians, all employed by Blue Cross.

A couple of days later I received a phone call with a job offer that I happily accepted. I later became the manager of the department. Over time I helped other inactive priests to achieve employment within the company – John, George and Brian are three names I recall.

Meanwhile, the headhunter became a true believer. He took all the inactive priests we could send to his company, and through him several obtained employment. One of them, in fact, became a headhunter in the same company.

I do not recall the number of inactive priests reconciled to the Church due to their association with Contact. However, I remember that a significant number informed me of demeaning treatment from the archdiocesan chancery staff. It reached the point where I phoned Bishop Joseph Brietenbeck to inform him of this manifest lack of charity. Within a week, changes became evident. A chancery insider contacted me with the news that the Bishop gathered the offending group into his office and castigated them for their lack of Christian behavior. Thereafter, the inactive priests were treated with dignity and respect.

After we moved to a home near the University of Detroit, Ruth became pregnant with our second-born, Patrick. It was at that time that a young priest, direct from Italy, appeared on our doorstep. He was looking for work and had heard about Contact. Through his very broken English we learned that he was now earning his living as a house painter. As Providence would have it, our recently arrived neighbors, Sheldon and Susan, needed the interior of their house painted. I suggested to Shel that he pay the young Italian in cash because he did not yet have his alien registration visa (green card); he had only just applied for it. In that way, also, there would be no taxes taken out from these earnings.

Shel began to roar with laughter. "Frank, we have only just been introduced and you don't know my background. I'm an auditor for the Internal Revenue Service in Detroit." I was shocked, stunned and speechless! Shel, without losing a beat, continued, "However, I understand the plight of this young man, and I do need to have our house painted. You've got a deal!" The Italian priest painter did an excellent job for them and they, in turn, referred him to their other friends. His visa arrived soon afterwards.

We became close friends with Susan and Shel and decided to ask them if they would look after our two boys if a mortal tragedy should occur to Ruth and me, since we had no living relatives in the United States. They accepted without hesitation. Shel, however, turned to me with his delightful Jewish humor and said, "There is only one stipulation, Frank. When your boys reach the age of eighteen, we will send them to a rabbinical college." Several times he jokingly reminded us of his future plans for our boys. To this day, we maintain communication with them.

As it happened, we too were painting our home when George and Julie visited us. She was born in Windsor, Ontario, and had been in the convent. George had been a leading cleric of the Maryknoll order in the state of New York. They had their hearts set on marriage, and George needed a job. It was the headhunter who had assisted me that gave George his first break in the working world. Later on, a position opened up at Blue Cross/Blue Shield, and I was able to recommend him for the job.

Over the years we lost track of them. Only recently did I learn that George and Julie are no longer together. He apparently returned to work as a lay missionary in Africa where formerly he had labored as a Maryknoll priest. Even as I write these words, a letter from George in Tanzania lies on my desk, describing the excellent work being accomplished among the poor in that region.

Later that year, Contact received an invitation from a local order of religious-teaching priests. We wondered why? The Superior, a most personable, early-middle-aged priest, often attended our monthly general meetings. Surprisingly, the letter contained a dinner/dance invitation for inactive priests and their wives to be held at the Holy Ghost Monastery. Upon reading it, I thought to myself, "How nice to be accepted by our brother priests." There were four priests living in the monastery at the time. Ruth and I had enjoyed their hospitality at a small dinner a month or two prior to receiving the group invitation. The majority of our members responded favorably to their gracious offer.

On the appointed evening, we appeared at their doorstep and were welcomed warmly. The evening's celebration consisted of a delicious meal, the soft music of our generation, and a light and jovial repartee. The dance, I recall, though limited due to lack of practice by most, was made enjoyable by the gracious hospitality of the four priests. We all left that evening emotionally filled with the milk of human kindness.

Within the next few months the rest of the story gradually unfolded. One by one the four Holy Ghost priests bid goodbye to their monastic lives to join the ranks of us who had already abandoned the active priesthood. The Superior was the last to leave. Our euphoria turned to sober reality at the news. In truth, the four had used us as pseudo-confirmation that life in the world was as soul-satisfying as life in the cloisters.

EIGHT

Acceptance and Rejection and Vatican Council II

The Lord gave and the Lord has taken away;
May the name of the Lord be praised!
    Job 1:21

Life gradually leveled out over the next four years. I was offered a new position leading to a promotion to management at Blue Cross/Blue Shield. Ruth was a stay-at-home wife and mother charged with the daily care and feeding of our two active sons. Contact had mainly achieved its faithfully adhered-to objectives. Its day-to-day operation grew over time and the original stigma attached to departing priests had slowly diminished. It was at that time that a professional opportunity came when we decentralized our entire department. I chose to move to Grand Rapids, Michigan, located on the western side of the state. The strong ties and associations with both active and inactive priests were reluctantly relaxed.

We settled in Jenison, a suburban community with a decidedly strong Christian Dutch Reformed flavor. Until the Meijer department store chain broke the mold, the overwhelming majority in Jenison observed Sunday as a day of rest. Washing one's car and mowing the lawn were frowned upon. Even the Jenison McDonald's proudly claimed it was the only one of its eateries that was closed on Sundays. For some older members of the community it seemed ideal, but in other ways, especially for the younger members of the community, the reins were held too tightly, where the boundaries of fresh air, sports, recreation and socializing proved overly restrictive. But overall, with churches filled, family activities given precedence, Sunday outings for relaxation – picnics in summer, sledding and skating in winter – Jenison was picture-perfect for *Currier and Ives*.

The Catholic population was probably not more than ten percent. We were surprised to learn that some of our neighbors had never had any Catholic friends nor did they associate with any Catholics. They tended to be friendly but only in a curious sort of way. We felt as if we were being observed somewhat like performers in a sideshow. Our question was: How could we, the parents, become part of the neighborhood? Our two boys had already made friends with other youngsters.

A short discussion with Ruth led to the following plan. We decided on an open house as the "new kids on the block" prior to Christmas, and invited all of our neighbors to join us. It was held on a sunny Sunday afternoon. We were both surprised and delighted that almost all the neighbors appeared on the scene. Apparently, there was strength in numbers for them.

Since going public with my religious background, I never again attempted to cover up my priestly status. I, therefore, was a double curiosity. Instinctively, according to Dutch custom, the women gathered in the living room and the men in the family room. Along with a generous supply of goodies, two bowls of punch had been prepared. The larger bowl, liberally spiked with Vodka, had a sign in front of it attesting to its potent authority. Like magic, so it seemed, it received by far the greater attention.

Within an hour, a noticeable social change took place. The men and women were animatedly "chatting it up" in various mixed groups. Stories of their Dutch heritage, proudly recounted, filled the air. Was it purely my imagination or did I detect a thickening of the Dutch accent as the day moved swiftly on? By afternoon's end, the gathering was judged a great success. Some, in fact, at time of departure, even inquired about when the next party would be held and to keep them on our invitational list.

We knew that we had been accepted into the neighborhood because, upon arriving home from work the following after-

noon, there in the driveway was a load of firewood. It was a gift
from Bob Ellis who lived across the road. He worked for the
forestry department in a supervisory capacity. That evening,
after dinner, he came over to help me stack it in the garage.
Whenever I ran short of fireplace wood I was to inform him and
another load would be delivered. The friendship has continued
between Bob and his wife, Phyllis, and us ever since. The ecumenical spirit was alive and well in Jenison!

There were so many solid Christian families we were privi-
leged to call neighbors. Herb and Marilyn Borst lived next door.
She was a dedicated nurse who specialized in the tender loving
care of "preemies." I recall one early Saturday summer morning
driving a pick-up truck, along with Herb and Bob Pyper, to a
mosquito-infested swamp. We were in search of six-foot evergreens to transplant to our back yards along our property lines.
It was hot and humid as we labored with pick and shovel, forc-
ing the earth to surrender our sought-after prizes. I remember
thinking to myself, covered with dirt and sweat, is God punish-
ing me for my many sins and misdemeanors? Today, the forty-
foot stately evergreens are a living testimony of our determination.

So often, in a newly flourishing neighborhood it is the children who bring the parents together. So it was with the Berrier
family! Patrick, our second born, was an elementary school
chum with Brian Berrier, and quickly became good buddies.
Each participated in hobbies, sports and school activities. Thus it
was that we met Hal and Diana Berrier. Hal is one of those men,
blessed with talent by God, to fix anything in a house that tended to malfunction. His wife, Diana, was one of the most devout
women I have ever encountered. It seemed their son and our son
were always either at their home or ours. To this day, whenever
Patrick flies in from Los Angeles, he phones Brian, now a successful salesman who recently celebrated his tenth year of being
cancer free. I can never recall those days without remembering
kind and gentle Hal and Diana Berrier for the love they lavished
on all their neighbors – both parents and children. What a fervent Christian couple Hal and Diana are! For over thirty years
we have continued to maintain a close relationship with them

and enjoy basking in their company. What an ideal way God chose to mold the characters of these two young boys, especially at a time when my religious practice was at low ebb!

For quality family living, Jenison was a town with few equals. It teemed with an abundance of children who could roam up and down the backyards since fences between neighbors were a rarity. There were no signs of litter. People took pride in the appearance of their houses and their property sitting on Jenison's many tree-lined streets. Quiet reigned on Sundays – church both in the morning and evening, much visiting among families and friends. The schools were neat and clean and the teachers, supported by interested parents, were dedicated to their work of stimulating the young minds and curiosity of their students. The local high school boasted an Olympic-sized swimming pool that was open to the local residents on most evenings. It took but five minutes to drive from our street to the many country lanes where the rich, sandy soil surrendered its vegetables and fruits in profusion. There were apple orchards, strawberry, raspberry and blueberry fields; onion, celery and lettuce farms everywhere we drove. No wonder, when we thought to retire, returning to Jenison was our first choice. Our sons heartily agreed with that decision.

In 1976 our town was in the process of forming its original Catholic presence through a new parish. Sunday Mass was initially celebrated in the local public school auditorium that attracted a surprisingly large number of faithful who began attending every Sunday. A building fund was quickly established with plans to begin the construction of a church within a year. Soon after his arrival, the pastor, armed with a list of his parishioners, distributed cards after each Mass for several Sundays. Each family was asked to complete a card indicating the activities in which we would like to participate as faithful parish members. I recall eagerly completing it, volunteering to teach courses in adult religious education.

As requested, I placed my card in the collection basket along with my offering. By mid-week I received an early evening telephone call from the pastor. He was effusive in expressing his delight that someone was interested in teaching Catholic religious education, since such teachers were extremely rare. He asked me, as was proper, about my credentials and experience. Without hesitation, I told him I was an inactive priest. His manner abruptly changed from warm enthusiasm to what sounded like panic – mixed with caution and dismay. It was similar to a blast of winter on a balmy summer afternoon. One moment I was a cohort, the next moment an enemy pounding at the fortress gate.

He asked how many knew of my priesthood. I told him I hid my defection from no one; but, in honesty, informed people that I did not blame the Church for my departure from it. Not only would he not use me to teach; the only activity he would allow was my attendance at Mass in his parish church. I was never again to bring up the subject of my background among his parishioners. For him, it would be the source of serious scandal. Thus, I was given my marching orders.

Unswerving, practicing Catholics have a profound reverence for their priests. They correctly perceived them as spiritual fathers who were God's chosen instruments to bring His graces to them through the Church's seven Sacraments, along with their teaching, preaching, counseling and the example of devout lives. A priest leaving his flock behind is a father deserting his spiritual family, causing sorrow, grief and scandal. At no time did this parish priest ask me why I left, where I worked, who my wife was, or if I had children. Nor did he recognize my priesthood by inviting me to the rectory for spiritual guidance. I was permanently assigned to his dead-letter box. Furthermore, he never directed any of his parishioners to visit us during the five years we lived in his parish.

During those years we devoted our time to raising our two sons, expanding our circle of friends, becoming more confident professionally, and, of course, studying. Over time, due to repeated inaction, missing Mass on Sunday ceased to bother my conscience. The sense of sin became less acute. Prayer became less frequent. Again, the world, the flesh and the devil were more in control due to my hurt pride. It is interesting to note, however, that our sons attended St. Pius Church in Grandville, the neighboring parish, for their religious instruction prior to First Communion, which both received at the proper time.

Feelings of resentment still rise to the surface – even to this day. However, when I reflect now, I poignantly understand the glaring error I made. I had prided myself on my ability to make proper distinctions. In the heat of my rejection, I failed to separate Christianity from Christendom – the Church from those who profess to be Christian. The Church, in its Head, who is Jesus in its teachings and practices, in its Sacraments and in its Saints, is holy. By no means do all of its members measure up to the ideals the Church espouses. My hurt pride tended to cloud my mind to this important reality.

I have alluded to Ruth, my wife, and to our two children, David and Patrick – but only slightly, in passing. You may legitimately inquire: How did the spiritual father of a parish compare with the human father of a family? Was it a successful transition? I might well be inclined to say, I am (was) a great exemplary head of the family until I recall the ten years I turned my back on the Catholic Church – I rarely saw the inside of a chapel or parish edifice. Further, my prayer life was neglected – almost, it seems, to the point of extinction. The bitterness I felt and the poor example I gave my family will always be a permanent personal source of hurt.

From a purely humanistic viewpoint, I did better. Ruth and I are fond of joking, especially with newfound friends, by my stating, "I have tried to convince Ruth over the years that I have never made a mistake in my life." She retorts, "And I made one!" Sometimes I, on such occasions, will glance at her quizzically to make sure that she is still kidding. I was almost forty-five when I became a father – Ruth is nearly fifteen years younger than me.

David and Patrick, born in April 1968 and August 1969, brought an immediate one-hundred-and-eighty degree turn into our lives. Over the years, I have tried to convince Ruth that all the good characteristics they have displayed were received through me. She doesn't buy it for a moment. Once when I informed her that she was impossible, she quickly replied, "Not really, I'm next to impossible." Our rule of thumb over the years has been to take our responsibilities seriously but take each other much less so. In other words, asking what can I give rather than what can I get. At the time it did not occur to me, but as I recall those years of family life, the special graces of the priesthood were very much alive in me. Once a priest, always a priest!

We, as a family, have always been supportive and close to each other. Much closer than most, I suspect. In some way, our two boys, as they grew older, sensed something different in our family discussions since everything was open and on the table. Consequently, during their high school years, they enjoyed bringing their young friends home to meet us. Ruth and I took time to sit and listen and reply to the comments and concerns of these youngsters. It came as a surprise to us to learn that many of them rarely, if ever, talked to their parents so openly.

Whenever possible, particularly during the summer months, I would take Ruth and the children with me on my overnight business trips. I would make certain that there was a swimming pool and recreational facilities at our hotel.

Ruth was a stay-at-home mom when the boys were young. She was there when they awakened and when they went to sleep. Somehow she succeeded in training me to volunteer my services by getting up in the middle of the night if one of the boys woke for whatever reason. My priesthood training in responding to middle-of-the-night sick calls was a great remote preparation.

The rearing of our sons was rarely difficult and, increasingly, we found it enjoyable to be in their company. Patrick once made the observation, "Dad, whenever we were out on a trip in the car, you never failed to stop at the parks on the way to our destination. You would stop the car and all of us would jump out and head for the swings and slides."

One sunny Saturday afternoon, while taking three-year-old David for a walk down Main Street in Royal Oak, an elderly gentleman passing by, smiled, and remarked, "Oh, it's a great day to be out with your grandson." I replied, also with a smile, "This is my older son, the younger one is home with his mother." When I saw the embarrassed look on his face, I assured him that I was in no way offended. I added, "It will be a great story to pass on to my friends."

My career progressed from health care management to medical clinic and hospital administration, to developing lectures in business ethics for Catholic executives of large corporations. Life was good on the surface but why did I often feel so uncomfortable? Like Nero, was I fiddling while Rome burned?

Even though I had discontinued attending Mass on Sundays, I continued to study, intrigued with the changes occurring in the structure of the Church since the close of Vatican Council II in 1965. My interest, however, did not prove to be the catalyst to return me to the fold. For a period of ten years, the changing face of the Church became increasingly more evident. If anything, it caused me to pull even further away. I would tell myself that simply going to church does not make you a Christian, anymore than standing in a cornfield would make me a scarecrow.

*   *   *   *

It might be instructive at this point to look at Vatican Council II with the hope that it will clarify some of the issues associated with it, as well as what is contained in parts of this book. In one sense it was a continuation of Vatican Council I, held between December 1869 and September 1870, the twentieth such council in the long history of the Roman Catholic Church. When the troops of King Victor Emmanuel seized Rome, the Council that defined the doctrine of Papal Infallibility came to an abrupt halt and never reconvened.

In a certain limited sense Vatican Council II, 1962 to 1965, continued to address some of the discontinued issues, especially regarding the power and limits of bishops gathered together or separately. In essence, it was a pastoral council rather than a doctrine-defining council convened by the much beloved Pope John XXIII. I recall reading that his gentleness was so recognized that the Russian Communist Politburo warned its adherents to say or write nothing detrimental about this dear man.

Following the death of Pope John XXIII, Giovanni Baptista Cardinal Montini was elected Pope Paul VI to rekindle the Council. Good Pope John XXIII, as he is benevolently known, in ways reminds me of St. Thomas Aquinas. It seems he was able to see only the good and the potential for good in other people. The oft-repeated tale concerning Thomas Aquinas is that after dinner one evening, the Dominican monks gathered at the window overlooking their farmland to play a trick on Thomas. They turned to him in a body, as he was about to arise from the table, and said, "Thomas, quickly come over here to the window, our cows are flying." The trusting Thomas rushed to the window-pane expecting to see these animals soaring in celestial flight. Instead, there they were in their usual evening mode contented-ly munching in the pasture. The young priests roared with laughter. It was then that Thomas turned to them and said, "I would rather think that cows could fly than that my brother monks could lie."

Pope John XXIII is recognized by two words: the first is *aggiornamento*, meaning "updating." It was his desire to bring a more pastoral, gentle, persuasive approach so as to make Roman Catholicism attractive to others. The second word is *metanoia*, a Greek word that conveys the meaning of a deep personal interi-or conversion or turning of the heart back toward God.

Unfortunately, there were Council participants who were eager to present an offsetting agenda. Their brand of updating was influenced by their own, less than edifying, lifestyles while their deep interior personal conversions were discarded. Such was the condition inherited by Pope Paul VI, a holy and brilliant man with precarious health problems and an overly cautious disposition. The so-called intelligentsia and members of acade-mia made up the Council's secular humanist splinter group. They were mostly associated with European and North American Catholic universities with the desire to separate the Church from its pre-Vatican II moorings, which they termed "restrictive" . In effect, they were out to offer radical changes in Roman Catholicism.

It might help our understanding of this Council by asking the questions: What were the documents developed during Vatican II? How did the traditional and the progressive elements interpret these documents?

Vatican II contained:

- Four Constitutions: the Sacred Liturgy, the Church itself, Divine Revelation and the Church in the modern world.

- Nine decrees: the meanings of social communication, Catholic Eastern Churches, Ecumenism, the pastoral office of the bishops in the Church, the training of priests, the up-to-date renewal of religious life, the apostolate of lay people, the Church's missionary activity, and the ministry and life of priests.
- Three declarations: Christian education, the relation of the Church to non-Christian religions and religious liberty.

By way of a passing remark, even after forty years many of these documents, generally speaking, have rarely been read and are insufficiently studied.

To place these documents in a more understandable context they speak of (1) the God revealed to Abraham as the Plenitude of Being worthy of our adoration; (2) man as a creature in his relationship to God; (3) man as a social being in community with each other; and (4) man as the caretaker of the world in both its cultural and environmental context. The intelligentsia perceived an opening for their progressive views and developed in their agenda what became known as the – watch this phrase – "hermeneutics of discontinuity." It simply means they arbitrarily threw out numbers one and two and concentrated on three and four. Due to their wallowing in secular humanism – that did away with the need for God – science and man's ability to rule himself and the world were paramount and sufficient. Coupled with their insufferable intellectual pride, they disengaged the Church's traditions and man's ascendancy to God through virtue. The vertical aspects of religion were shoved aside from the horizontal aspects that dealt with religion on a purely secular plane.

All ideas, of course, have consequences. It was only much later that we realized how well their individual lifestyles and intellectual pride influenced their progressive thinking.

Unfortunately, a significant number of the bishops who attended the Council in a somewhat bewildered state went along with the euphoria of a new Church. They returned home after the Council to pursue this stunted progressive agenda for their flocks. The intelligentsia took the high ground by going to the secular media, the entertainment industry and the Catholic universities to advance their agenda, to shuck off the old pre-Vatican Council disciplines in favor of unfettered freedom.

The seeds of these destructive plans were born decades prior to the Council. Coupled with the sexual revolution in the mid-1960s, the results were and continue to be disastrous. Let me give you three little blips that have personally occurred during the past few months. A nun who never wears her religious habit works as a social worker and is really quite likeable said to me recently, "I love to hear you speak in Latin. I realize that my order is dying, but meanwhile, I am having a ball." My sister, Agnes, who had been a member of a religious group, taught in the separate school system, became principal of a school and finally left the convent when many of the sisters moved into apartments, devastating the community life of the sisters. Agnes now lives a life of sanctity in her own home. She told me the other day that her order has not received a single new vocation in five years. The beautiful convent and the sisterly love that surrounded the dedicated teaching order of sisters will now become a nursing home.

The third event appeared in our local newspaper. Our bishop was quoted on planning to move his chancery office from its present quarters closer to the cathedral church. Upon reading the article, I could not help but think of moving the chairs on the deck of the Titanic. The Church has not been decimated, which means reduced by ten, rather it has been devastated and reduced by probably eighty percent or more. Perhaps today, twenty-five percent of our people really believe in the Real Presence of Jesus in the Blessed Sacrament. Ours is a day when community flourishes – we hold hands at Mass, Eucharistic ministers invade the Sanctuary, the altar has become a table, the Eucharist has become a meal rather than a Sacrifice – it's party time – let's wear our casual clothes to greet each other since our Eucharist King is far removed from our presence while the banal songs tend to celebrate the singers rather than the Son of God. Who needs to spend a few moments in Thanksgiving after Mass? We are a closed circle celebrating each other with the priest and the people facing each other rather than facing in the same direction in adoration of our Eucharistic King. The sense of the sacred in many of our churches has all but disappeared. The progressives have won the day but God's providence still remains the factor that will turn the tide to renew our spirit and to redeem our souls. I still hear the voice of Pope John Paul II, "Do not be afraid." The *metanoia* of Pope John XXIII is still to be realized through contrition, confession, forgiveness and amendment of life in the heart of each person.

What is written here is but a brief digression to attempt to throw a small ray of understanding on today's institutional church. Actually, there are now two churches – one the Roman Catholic Church, and the other an American Catholic Church. To which one do I belong?

Pope Benedict XVI has been presented with a formidable task and is most deserving of our most fervent prayers. With the grace of God all things are possible. Be uplifted by the words written in II Chronicles 7:14: "If my people, which are called by my name, shall humble themselves, and pray, and seek my face, and turn from their wicked ways; then will I hear from heaven, and will forgive their sin, and will heal their land." Make no mistake these are God's words, His promise to us. He will supply the wind if we will but hoist the sail. We know now what we must do. The critical question is: Do we have the will to carry it out in our lives?

Let me conclude this chapter with a quotation from Paul Johnson, a wise and perceptive English historian. He wrote this about the Church:

The people of the Catholic faith value it not because it is yielding but because it is inflexible; not because it is open-minded but because it is sure; not because it is adaptive and protean but because in essentials it is always the same. It is the one fixed point in a changing world.

Catholicism is not a market-place religion. It is not in business to count heads or to take votes. In its sacred economy, quantitative principles do not apply. Dogma and morals are not susceptible to guidance by public opinion. The truth is paramount and it must be the naked truth, presented without cosmetics and exercises in public relations.

The Catholic Church has not survived and flourished over two millennia by being popular. It has survived because what it taught was true. The quest for popularity, as opposed to the quest for truth, is bound to fail.

NINE

The Lutheran and the Muslim

For there is no difference between Jew and Gentile –
The same Lord is Lord of all and richly
Blesses all who call on him.
     Romans 10:12

John Parker, a business acquaintance, who was heading up a cancer research group focusing on the immune system, asked me to join him. A physician at the local Veterans' Hospital had produced some promising breakthroughs in cancer treatment and had sought John's help. Through an arrangement with the University of Michigan, researchers were brought into the program.

Since Canada had a total government-funded health insurance program, John looked in that direction for both funding and execution of this promising cancer prevention treatment. As a Canadian, John wondered if I had any connections that could be used to advance his research. So it was that I became actively involved in John's project.

My former association with the Ontario Department of Health drew a complete blank. Then I remembered a seminary classmate who was now an auxiliary bishop in Toronto. He was also a board member of St. Michael's Hospital in that city. I telephoned the bishop's secretary who set up a meeting for us. The 200-mile trip from Detroit to Toronto, with John at the wheel, took place in record time. Driving with John at the wheel was always an adventure. He had superb reflexes and, in spite of his speedy habits, at no time did I experience any discomfort. He had been a test-pilot trainer during World War II and a graduate engineer. I told John that a lamb was the only thing that could make a 'ewe' turn, since he was a master at such maneuvers.

The bishop met us in the hallway of the administrative section of the hospital where a board meeting had just concluded. Instinctively, as an old seminary friend, I put both my arms out to clasp him by the shoulders. Just as instinctively, I felt him pulling back. His opening pompous remark was, "Well, Frank, what is it that you are after? What favor are you looking from me this time?" Initially, I was unsure of what he meant. Then it came to me – I had contacted St. Augustine's Seminary to obtain proof of my graduation plus a transcript of my grades. Bishop Wall, as Dean of Studies of the Seminary at that time, had affixed his signature to my graduation document. This apparently was the "favor" to which he had alluded. These papers had been requested by Blue Cross prior to my hire, which, as previously mentioned, led to a number of needy inactive priests obtaining employment. I decided it was not worth bringing this up to the bishop during the time of this visit; I judged this to be a private matter. His attitude toward me during the interview continued on the cool side. By this time, the pattern of such clerical rejection was no longer a surprise or source of anguish to me, only a moderate irritation. The research, however, did interest him, which led to doors being opened for us.

As we left the hospital, John, not a Catholic, although delighted over the Canadian introductions, casually mentioned how much warmer it was outside than within the building.

My association with cancer research continued for two years, due mainly to some of my connections with health insurance providers, administrative hospital personnel and physician friends. At this time, the mid-1980s, I was living again in the suburbs of Detroit, there having completed my chapter with Blue Cross/Blue Shield.

The biggest favor John Parker did for me was to introduce me to a remarkable man with the arresting name of Arvid Jouppi. Arvid, a Lutheran and a proud Finn, had been a senior member of a New York stock exchange company and had moved to Detroit to form his own company. I can't fix the precise date of our first meeting, but I do know that he was then a recognized world-class expert of automotive economic trends. On any given weekday, Arvid could be heard being interviewed either on radio or television for his analysis of the auto industry. We formed a special lasting friendship, which, in all likelihood, had much to do with my priesthood.

In Detroit a group of fourteen or fifteen distinguished business executives had formed a roundtable of like-minded persons. Their purpose was to be a sounding board to those in the car industry. The chairman of this group who was aware of my friendship with Arvid asked me if I would invite him to be a member of their roundtable. I did so when he and I met next for breakfast. Arvid graciously agreed to join the group.

Arvid was inducted into the roundtable, and in a remarkably short time the chairman began receiving requests from all over the world for information about the organization. Such was the esteem in which Arvid was held.

On a regular basis, either Arvid or I would call each other to arrange for breakfast at a convenient restaurant. During these sessions the topic of the automotive industry rarely surfaced. Our conversations centered on religion, on the goodness and mercy of God as personified in the human nature of Jesus. Always before beginning our meal, we would begin with bowed heads and folded hands. Arvid would pray without fanfare and with no sense of false piety to acknowledge God's presence in our midst, to thank him for his generosity, and to acknowledge our total dependence on Him. Rarely, have I met a more Christlike person.

Was the purpose of these meals purely to talk of these things? By no means, Arvid truly lived his faith – as I came to realize over time.

Regularly, on Saturday mornings, Arvid and his wife would deliver food and clothing to some of the poorest sections of Detroit on his own initiative. He told me of one such Saturday visit. The area in which he chose to visit was not considered the safest section of the city. In the process of taking food and articles of clothing to an impoverished family, he happened to glance out from the second-floor tenement window. A large black man was seen looking intently at Arvid's car. The thought flashed through his mind – would the car be stripped by the time he was through with his visit? Ashamed, he put the thought out of his head. When he left the building in the company of his wife, the man had not moved from his spot in front of the car. Arvid was unsure of what was occurring. His uncertainty quickly was clarified.

"Mr. Jouppi," the man explained, "the families that live here are grateful for all you do for them. I stopped by to thank you. The way I'm doing it, sir, is that I'm guarding your car. I'm also here to protect you from harm. I'm sure you are aware, Mr. Jouppi, that this is not the safest area in Detroit."

Arvid admitted feeling a rush of relief and gratitude. From that time on, each Saturday, the same or another man would be present to guard his vehicle week after week.

Arvid, although a Lutheran, never hesitated to remind me of my own priestly responsibilities. Since he was eager to lead by his own good example, it was much more palatable to react positively to his words. Arvid was older than me by a few years. In many ways he took the place of an older brother. Arvid's friend and associate since 1960, Forrest von Foerster, also a Lutheran, has remarked more than once, "Arvid Jouppi is the only truly Christian person I have ever met." Years later I learned that Arvid gave away to charity from eighty to ninety percent of all he earned.

When he became seriously ill, I drove to his home in Grosse Pointe to visit him. It was a sturdy, attractive house matching other dwellings in this upscale neighborhood. I had never before visited his home. His wife welcomed me at the door. There was Arvid lying in bed in their living room. Throughout the whole of the downstairs, his house had almost a threadbare appearance, with few of the so-called nicer things in life. The interior was in startling contrast to the neighborhood. This dear couple, I came to realize, had given most of their worldly possessions away.

As soon as I saw Arvid's face, I realized they had saved their best – their vast love for God and for each other. I will never forget his sick room which was warm with that endearing love. I went there to console my brother in Christ. I left with far more than what I was able to bring. He died shortly afterwards. Daily I pray for his loving, generous soul. May Arvid rest in eternal peace with his dear Lord!

Through my acquaintance with John Parker and a network of automotive people, a second consulting position was offered to me. Hesham Roushdy, an engineer with the Ford Motor Company who developed the first automatic transmission for the Ford Escort, had taken early retirement to form his own business – Inmart Corporation.

My initial visit to his house to begin our business association was unforgettable. His son was outside playing with his little sister in the driveway. As I emerged from my car, this youngster, around age ten, picked up a baseball bat and stepped in front of his charge. He was immediately *engarde* against any unannounced stranger. It began to look like a standoff. Fortunately, Hesham appeared on the porch, took in the scene and immediately ordered his son to put his stout cudgel away. Upon being introduced, I congratulated this young man for his brave stance, and I have thought often since, "If only all young boys acted in such a chivalrous manner in protecting their little sisters!"

Hesham was a Muslim deeply immersed in his faith. His most oft-repeated Arabic phrase was – translated into English – "God willing."

We immediately set in motion a strategy to interest Mid-Eastern businessmen in purchasing autos through our emerging enterprise. Hesham was born in Egypt and was a personal friend of Anwar Sadat, former President of Egypt, who was later assassinated. My role was to develop the necessary literature and business correspondence for communication with people in Saudi Arabia, Kuwait, the United Arab Emirates and Egypt. Hesham's activities included the procurement of autos at the local level.

Some months into operations, Hesham, who, in quiet moments, was often eager to discuss Islamic and Christian beliefs, invited me to attend a Friday night meeting at a mosque in East Dearborn, Michigan. This was something entirely new in my experience. I quickly accepted his kind offer.

On Friday evening, Hesham, along with his wife and children, drove me to the mosque. Inside the main door and to the right was the mosque proper, where several men could be seen on their knees in prayer. I was quickly informed that this area was unavailable to me; it was reserved exclusively for the followers of Islam. Inside the large auditorium there must have been considerably more than 1,000 people present – men, women and children – all Muslims. I was the lone exception.

Their hospitality can only be described as overwhelming. Dates, grapes, feta cheese, pita bread, cakes and cookies of all sorts were pressed upon me. Man after man came up to introduce himself. In no time, I lost the sense of being a decided minority. It was impossible not to notice the women remaining in the background and the very large number of well-behaved children. The sounds of laughter could be heard throughout the large auditorium. The sense of family permeated the air, with both parents openly showing strong affection for their children. If the "battle of the cradle," as it was once termed in Catholic Quebec, took place today, the followers of Islam would win hands down.

The thought occurred to me – was I observing the twilight of European influence that had for five centuries dominated Western thought and culture?

Hesham and I worked many long hours setting up business arrangements with agents of auto distributors in Kuwait. Our efforts appeared to be ready to pay off handsomely. We had hundreds of autos to sell, the prices were right and the Kuwaiti contacts were eager to do business. Shipping schedules had long before been arranged, with all necessary documents in place for overseas commerce.

The week before shipping was to occur, Iraq invaded Kuwait – our business came to a crashing halt!

While hostilities raged in the Middle East, Hesham took time out, and I found myself at loose ends, unemployed. The thought of retirement presented itself. A few months later, I learned that Hesham had taken a trip to Egypt, the country of his birth. While swimming in the Red Sea, he had a heart attack and drowned. God willing, may the Lord have mercy on his gentle soul!

Many of us who profess to be Catholics are acutely spoiled. God has so showered us with his abundant graces that we have become complacent and apathetic to the Sacraments, devotions and prayers. We sit in our first-class seats as spectators, passively watching the human parade go by. It has been noted and stated many times that scores of our charged-up Catholics are both converts and reverts to the faith. These are the people who truly appreciate the many channels of grace the Catholic Church offers to all of us.

Two such outstanding converts are John Henry Cardinal Newman and Gilbert Keith Chesterton, both of whom are being considered for canonization. There is a host of others that could also be mentioned. Without going into the lives of either, there are two noticeable features that rise to the surface. Newman, who was severely persecuted after his conversion, spoke often of *cor ad cor loquens*, which translates "heart speaking to heart." Chesterton, as his cause for sainthood proceeds, is spoken of as "the saint who laughed his way into heaven."

As I reflect on my deep and abiding friendships with both Arvid Jouppi, the Lutheran, and Hesham Roushdy, the Muslim, both of these traits emerge in my recollections. In a short time our hearts opened in friendship to each other and in a most comfortable brotherly manner we spoke from the depth of our souls "heart speaking to heart."

All the while, our conversations were liberally punctuated with laughter, banter and good humor, tall tales and manly teasing. We tended not to take ourselves too seriously as we seriously sought sanctity from each other.

These two guidelines should, I estimate, be used in the development of friendships whether with Catholics, Protestants, Jews or Muslims. Those of us who reach our eternal reward might well be surprised who we will meet in God's celestial kingdom. Sometime, look up a poem entitled *Abou Ben Adhem*, penned by James Leigh Hunt. The final line states, "And, lo! Ben Adhem's name led all the rest." The poem will help you to understand why. Once again, Arvid and Hesham, I pray for the repose of your dear souls. Please pray for me.

TEN

The Desolate City:
The Muggeridge Influence

For here we do not have an enduring city,
But we are looking for the city that is to come.
Hebrews 13:14

One spring afternoon in 1989, I stopped off at my local library. The time had arrived, I decided, to shake off the cares and troubles of the world and settle down to a life of relative peace and tranquility. What I needed was to relax with a good book. As I fingered my way through the stacks, I had a vague recollection of someone recommending *The Desolate City* by Anne Roach Muggeridge. I brought it home that evening, opened its pages and I was shocked.

Her book dealt with Catholic Canada. As a native Canadian, I felt hers was a subject that I knew something about. Yet, I was blissfully ignorant of the precipitous downhill slide in the life of the institutional Catholic Church in Canada. For the previous ten years, my association with the institutional church had been limited. I had put it on hold.

According to her, this descent all began with the reforms of the Second Vatican Council in the 1960s. Recall, that Pope John XXIII, who presided over these historic proceedings, often used the Greek word *metanoia*. *Metanoia* means to change one's mind, to repent, to be converted. In its true context, it implies a deep interior change of heart from sin to the practice of virtue.

Metanoia was the first obligation that Saint Peter demanded of his audience on Pentecost Sunday, and it is considered essential to the pursuit of Christian perfection. All of us know how much easier and more pleasant it is to attempt to change others than it is to attempt to change ourselves. Unfortunately, I'm afraid, *metanoia* came to be erroneously applied to the externals of the institutional Church rather than to its interior disposition.

Since the close of Vatican II in 1965, and over the next two generations, Christendom has reeled from one external change to another: the authority of the Pope was challenged; church buildings were redesigned (inside and out); the rubrics of the Mass took on a new format (varying from one parish to another). Priests' schedules were changed in many parishes from total availability to nine-to-five office hours. The sacramental aspects of the priesthood gave way to a pastoral ministry. Confessions were cut to the bone. Religious habits were tossed aside in favor of secular attire. Lay activity in the Church became focused and fixed around the sanctuary rather than in the community.

All these external progressive changes indeed occurred while Pope John XXIII invited all nations to repentance. Meanwhile, the Western world had begun its descent into the sex-drugs-and-rock-and-roll era. The influence on the structure of the Church was devastating. Almost immediately the deterioration of the religious disciplines – once so admired in Catholic seminaries, religious orders and in priestly practices – became evident. The results were obvious – a collapse in religious vocations and an exodus from the priesthood and sisterhood.

Politics is in largest part a function of culture; at the heart of culture is morality; and at the heart of morality are the ultimate truths we call religion. There is hardly any discussion of a serious nature that does not include one or more of these four functions. Since the majority of our Catholic religious leaders, with a total adherence of over sixty million Catholics in the United States, spinelessly allowed a materialistic culture to overwhelm its battlements, we find ourselves in such a sorry state today fairly wallowing in decadence. This tidal wave of secular changes washed over the moral foundations of the Church and left its religious standards reeling, if not impotent.

I learned that Anne was the wife of John Muggeridge. He is the son of the famous and beloved British Broadcasting Corporation (BBC) commentator, Malcolm Muggeridge. In his later years, Malcolm became a convert to Catholicism. The following sentiments, which may well have influenced his daughter-in-law to write *The Desolate City*, were penned by Malcolm in his Foreword to a book entitled *Jesus Rediscovered*, prior to his entrance into the Catholic Church. These meaningful words reflected my own sentiments at that time and are well worth reproducing here.

The old pagan gods were all represented in terms of earthly power and wealth and pulchritude – gleaming and mighty and lascivious. The cross for the first time revealed God in terms of weakness and lowliness and suffering; even, humanly speaking of absurdity. He was seen thenceforth in the image of the most timid, most gentle and most vulnerable of all living creatures – a lamb. Agnus Dei! So they have been joyously singing through the centuries. Agnus Dei!

It is very difficult for me to explain that the more enchanted I become with the person and teaching of Christ, the further away I feel from all institutional Christianity, especially this particular institution, which, as I consider, is now racing at breakneck speed to reproduce all the follies and fatuities of Protestantism, and will surely before long arrive at the same plight, with crazed clergy, empty churches and total doctrinal confusion.

Malcolm, as a Protestant, here is voicing his concerns about where he perceived the Church of England and the post-Vatican II American Catholic Church was heading. Mr. Muggeridge certainly hits a nerve – a sensation that many of us are experiencing today. Among the influences that kept Malcolm on course were letters of encouragement, such as one from a monk whom he had befriended. The monk wrote him, "Every morning at 5:00 A.M., before I go to offer the Holy Sacrifice, as a small token of my gratitude to you, I ask our beloved Savior to be good to you and to those dear to you. I will continue to do that for whatever short time remains before I meet Him face-to-face." This good and pious monk was able to discern the truth and goodness for which Malcolm was searching and in his kindness responded to that need.

These words remind me of the motto of St. Augustine's Seminary that, translated from its Latin inscription, states, "Let charity alone reign like the sun." If only we would inscribe those words into the very fiber of our being!

To these words of comfort, Malcolm responds, "No one human being could possibly do another a more precious favor than this, such gestures flood the whole universe with light."

His words inspire readers differently. They flood my mind with truth, and their goodness reaches into the deep recesses of my heart. It is God who shows us the deepest meaning of that most over-used and abused of words: to love is to give oneself, to share oneself, to be opening and welcoming towards the other, to reach out towards the other in selfless sacrifice. It is in imitation of our God who is Love itself, a God Who gives and shares Himself with us. When we ponder the inner mystery of the Blessed Trinity, three divine persons in one God, this is above all what the doctrine seeks to proclaim. The Father continues to create us throughout our entire existence as an ongoing process. He sends His only Son to redeem us. Jesus suffers and dies for us. The Holy Spirit gathers up the infinite ocean of graces won for us on the Hill of Calvary and bestows them upon us in order to make us more Christ-like; so that the Son in turn may as our elder brother take us home to His heavenly Father. Such is the economy of our salvation.

Now, back to Anne Muggeridge, a faithful and feisty defender of the faith in today's ongoing battle for souls. Her book – as none other did – opened my eyes to the plight of the Catholic Church throughout the length and breadth of Canada. What was true of the institutional Church in Canada was true also of the Church in the United States. When I finished reading the book, I was stunned and angry: stunned at what had occurred because I had been out of touch for many years, and suddenly angry with myself for my immaturity, my laziness, my pride.

I found the telephone number of the Muggeridge family, who live a mere 40 miles from my place of birth, and called her. Anne answered. It took about thirty minutes of an honest, heartwarming conversation to make me realize where my quarrel was and where my focus needed to be. It was not with Christianity but with Christendom.

Some years later, Jerry Urbik, a good friend, also reminded Ruth not to be misled by those who, whether priests or lay persons, profess to be Catholic, but whose lives and actions point to values anything but Catholic. Archbishop Sheen made the observation more than once that there were not a thousand people in the United States who hate the Catholic Church, but there are millions who hate what they mistakenly think the Catholic Church is.

I sorrow over my own lack of commitment during those years when I pulled back from the practice of my faith. At the same time, I thank God for His patience and mercy towards me and for the many prayers said on my behalf by those who genuinely love me.

A few years later, I had the good fortune to meet Anne and John Muggeridge in Toronto. John appeared much as I imagined his father to be, both in looks and temperament. Anne is tiny, but only on the outside; her spirit is that of a giant.

Our family began attending Mass once again after seeking out a good spiritual director – not always easy to find. My sons and I made sincere contrite confessions. Ruth still resisted becoming a Catholic. The hurts and bad examples were still felt deeply within her.

I discovered that the sense of the sacred at Mass was difficult to detect, the participation of the laity almost nonexistent, the music trivial, mundane and secular, and churches half-filled. I noted that emphasis was now on the pastoral concerns of the priest. The essential sacramental character of the priesthood was on the back burner. Consequently, sin was rarely mentioned; it was, I suppose, not considered a pastoral topic. The liturgy was re-routed in an attempt to make it "meaningful," with lay liturgical experts invading every crook, crevice and corner of the sanctuary. *The Desolate City* was indeed an apt title for Anne Muggeridge's book.

The question logically needs to be asked: What caused this transformation in the institutional Church? Further study and research led me to the answer. There were two diametrically opposed main forces at work in the Church during the mid-1960s, plus a third force lurking in the background.

To better understand what was occurring, we may look to Mother Teresa. Her day and that of her Missionaries of Charity began with a very early morning approach to God on their knees, and went from that vertical posture to a horizontal posture in the poorest sections in the streets of Calcutta to focus on the most destitute and needy. This was the model envisioned by Pope John XXIII for peace and justice in the world. He knew there could never be lasting justice without a genuine love of God overflowing from every human being to his or her neighbor. Justice without charity is cruelty; charity without justice is weakness.

God is love whose mercy prevails until the end of time when His justice becomes manifested and all evils will be rectified. Good will be rewarded and its absence will be punished. Now is the time given to us to store up treasures in heaven.

The second force, generally composed of Catholic theologians, was present in Rome during Vatican II to assist the bishops gathered in the Eternal City. Michael Davies, the prominent English convert to Catholicism with close connections to the Vatican, informs us of the secret progessive, liberalized agenda of a select leading group of dissident theologians. This group included Karl Rahner, S.J. of Germany, Edward Schillebeeckx of Belgium, Hans Küng of Germany and the well-known, well-traveled Joseph Cardinal Suenens of Belgium. As this last mentioned prelate was traveling about the globe, basking in the adulation of his supporters, Belgium was slowly sinking into materialistic relativism. Perhaps, had he stayed home and remained faithful to his high calling, that portion of Europe might well have weathered the upheaval of the Church.

The true purpose of a theologian is to support and clarify the doctrines and practices of the Church – not always an easy task. This time, the theologians wanted more – more power, more recognition, more appreciation and, above all, more freedom to throw off what they perceived as a centuries-old encrustation of outdated patriarchal shackles. *Metanoia* to them meant wholesale changes in the institutional Church. In place of a sacramental priesthood, they opted for a pastoral one. Pope John Paul II,

Joseph Cardinal Ratzinger, Avery Cardinal Dulles and St. Thomas Aquinas all have consistently insisted that the essence of the priest is to be found in his sacramental character where he acts as the conduit of God's grace.

Nowhere was the effect of the theologians' misguided sense of *metanoia* more devastating than on the sisters and nuns. Community life and religious habits were traded for apartments and secular attire. Social justice issues took front and center over teaching children about the love of God as seen through His Divine Son. Indeed, the theologians had a well-planned agenda. Once they had the bit in the mouth of the Church, there was no holding them back. Most of the bishops who had brought them along to Rome were aghast and, sad to relate, often intimidated. The fallout from this is to be seen in the extreme high percentage of chancery offices and parishes throughout the nation who employ decidedly liberal-minded and progressive personnel. Even in the United States Council of Catholic Bishops (USCCB), their offices are awash with those who espouse the principles of the American Catholic Church – married and women priests; homosexuality, contraception and abortion rights. Control and authority were breached and wrested from the bishops by their theologian assistants.

The theologians had a field day with the television, radio and print secular media that eagerly sought them out (rather than the bishops) for interviews. Alas, many bishops, who either secretly favored the progressive philosophy or were short on courage and conviction, affected a political stance. Putting moistened forefingers to the wind to discern its direction, they quietly surrendered and some even joined the ranks of the progressive brigade.

The third force at work in the mid-1960s that encouraged the theologians to further seek to liberalize their thinking was the hedonism of the baby boomers, feminism and "The Pill." The battle was now joined. Suddenly, in the institutional Catholic Church there were two alternative teaching authorities, not parallel but instead divergent. There was the ancestral voice of Rome drowned out by a strident voice demanding a progressive church. Infected with the materialism that followed on the heels of World War II, most Catholics opted for the liberalized version, and so it has continued for two generations.

It is important that the following concept be well understood and grasped. The soundness of what we believe absolutely depends upon and is influenced by the soundness of how we live out our moral and spiritual lives. Throughout history this has been true of saints and sinners, the orthodox believer and the heretic. Our ideas, without exception, grow out of our personal lives. They influence what we believe about God the Father, His Son, and the Church that He founded through the power of the Holy Spirit.

ELEVEN

Legatus: Ambassadors for God

We are therefore Christ's ambassadors,
As though God were making his appeal through us.
      II Corinthians 5:20

My retirement in 1988 permitted me to increase the time I spent reading and to widen the scope of what I read. I began to notice the term *Legatus* (Latin for legate or ambassador) cropping up in both religious and secular publications. Father Michael Scanlan, President of Franciscan University at Steubenville, suggested the title *Legatus* to Thomas Monaghan as the name of his elite organization. Tom was the founder of the immensely successful Domino's Pizza and, at that time, owner of Detroit Tigers baseball team. The members of Legatus consider themselves to be ambassadors for Christ in the world of business.

To qualify for this elite organization, most members have to be presidents, chief executive officers or managing partners in sizeable, successful companies. Membership also requires that they are dedicated, practicing Catholics. Members' wives are automatically full-fledged members of Legatus. The organization is designed to assist talented, visible, influential Catholic leaders to promote and foster Catholic values, principles and ethics in the business world. Members are encouraged to be visibly active in their local parishes and to offer their leadership and professional resources.

Thomas Angott, President of the Detroit Pure Milk, was a founding member of Legatus. Several months after intently listening to an array of inspiring speakers at their monthly meetings, Tom decided to apply Legatus' concepts to his company. It was a union shop that conducted annual labor negotiations on a rigid, formal take-no-prisoners basis. Neither the company nor union representatives would give an inch without undue force being exerted.

Tom told me this story:

Legatus had begun in 1987. As the time for annual labor negotiations approached, he said, he could feel the predictable hostility building in the air. The same issues surfaced – better wages, expanded benefits and humane working conditions. He listened quietly to the union's list of concerns. When it came time for him to respond, he replied in a surprisingly gentle voice that many of the concerns were legitimate and would be immediately addressed. There was dead silence in the conference room. Mind you, he was not about to give away the store. The points, he stressed, were justice tempered by genuine Christian love leading to dignity and respect for all his employees.

It was the beginning of a new era for his company. "So profits will be down," he said to himself. "You can't win 'em all!"

Gradually, over the next few weeks, when arriving for work in the morning, he noticed his employees acknowledging his presence with cheery hellos as he walked through to his office. What a startling contrast to the dead, cold silence with which he was formerly subjected. He began to look forward to these increasingly friendly morning encounters. As the year ahead took shape, he was astounded to observe the net profits increasing.

Legatus has a regular monthly format observed by all chapters – chapters that gradually surfaced in the largest cities in the country. Each chapter must appoint a spiritual director who would be available at all monthly meetings for Confessions, to celebrate Mass for the group and for spiritual consultations. Chapter meetings, which begin after Mass, include a half-hour social gathering, dinner and a speaker, followed by a stimulating question-and-answer period.

My association with Legatus can be traced to my familiarity with many of the great papal social encyclicals that addressed capitalism, labor unions and the right to organize, plus the dignity of all persons, including working class laborers. These papal letters on social justice began with Pope Leo XIII at the end of the 19th century, following the Industrial Revolution. I decided to make a telephone call (or two, or three) to Legatus' national headquarters in Ann Arbor, Michigan. The real purpose of my calls was simply to offer suggestions to the fledgling group in what I perceived as a clear direction.

Exactly what it was I said that captured the attention of the executive director, I'm not quite sure. However, one spring morning in 1989, I received a telephone call asking if I would drop into her office the following week. On the day and time appointed, I found myself on Legatus' doorstep, idly wondering, "Have I finally got myself in over my head?"

I was ushered into a room to meet the five-person staff. They quickly revealed their interest in my Canadian roots. For some time Legatus had been on the lookout for someone to develop a chapter in Toronto and, thereby, become an international organization. Plans also were underway for chapter development in Mexico.

I was thoroughly grilled, then asked to take a chair outside and read from among a large selection of mostly Catholic periodicals. Fifteen minutes later I was called before the entire staff. The director offered me a position to initiate plans for chapters in Canada, beginning with Toronto.

I needed time to pray on the offer and talk it over with Ruth. As surprised as I was, she told me in no uncertain terms that sticking my nose into other people's business usually leads to trouble. Besides, she reminded me, smiling sweetly, "How about our own personal plans?" After I reviewed the pros and cons, I decided to put our retirement plans on hold, and accepted the position.

Prior to my active involvement, the director of Legatus invited Ruth and me to dinner, in order to meet the organization's sole Canadian member. Terry Coles, president of a popular radio station in Windsor, Ontario, belonged to the Detroit/Ann Arbor chapter. And what do you think I discovered at that dining table? Not only had Terry, as a youngster, served Mass for my uncle, Father Vincent Morgan, in Acton, Ontario; he had also been the altar server for the Masses I had celebrated whenever, prior to my leaving the active priesthood, I had visited my uncle!

Indeed, it's a small world!

My new venture was a tough nut to crack. Except for a few brief visits, I had been away from Toronto for nearly twenty-five years. There was one person who could get the ball rolling – Terry Coles. He was an ardent Catholic who had connections across the entire country in both radio and television. Yes, he had contacts in Toronto! He knew Bill Cooke, owner and president of Enterprises. Bill had televised Pope John Paul II when he graced Toronto with a visit. It was the shining moment of Bill's entire career.

This international adventure began to look like a job made in heaven for me and I eagerly looked forward to working with Bill. I thought to myself, "How good God is to a poor sinner like me!"

Information on the scope and purpose of Legatus was faxed to Bill Cooke's office in preparation for a meeting with him the following week. Then it was that I found myself in his office near Yonge and Bloor Streets in the heart of metropolitan Toronto. It was only a few short blocks from St. Michael's College, affiliated with St. Augustine's Seminary, my alma mater.

Bill was all I could have hoped for – a tall, charming forty-plus-year-old with boundless energy, a personality to match and immense good humor. He was surprisingly enthusiastic about Legatus. Canada lagged economically behind the United States with much greater rates of unemployment. He felt that Legatus, through financial and advisory assistance, might well be a spur to some of his business friends and associates. His own television business was thriving because of his leadership, but he was not unaware of the opportunities offered from positive publicity through Legatus.

I arrived to find an office with all the necessary accoutrements waiting for me. Bill had put some thought into the organization and presented me with a list of fifteen or more potential members. This was my kind of guy! His infectious enthusiasm set me into high gear.

By week's end, we had a spiritual director plus a back-up priest, arrangements for our Confessions and Masses at St. Michael's Cathedral chapel, and a room for catered receptions and dinners. After these dinners a special guest would speak on various religious and cultural topics.

For two years I immersed myself in Legatus, working to expand membership, improve the quality of the meetings and act in the capacity of unofficial chaplain for some of the members, spouses and even their children.

The wives of these executives were as enthusiastic as their husbands in many cases. They were forming lasting bonds of friendship and developing a more appreciative understanding of their husbands' business activities and challenges, many of which the wives had not been aware.

The Basilian Fathers at St. Michael's College, some of whom I still knew, graciously opened their dining- and meeting-room facilities for us, which were ideal. They offered me personally one more favor – a room in the priests' dormitory whenever I was in Toronto. This kindness I gratefully accepted and will never forget.

In 1991, nearly two years after beginning my work at Legatus, a male staff employee asked to talk with me privately. It was during the week following a national convention in Chicago, which had been attended by chapter members from across the country.

This concerned young man informed me in an embarrassed, hesitant, faltering fashion that a chaplain had made sexual advances towards him. They had been assigned accommodations in the same hotel room. He slowly spelled out the details. Horrified, shocked and scandalized, he fled from the priest and the room. Would I handle the matter for him since he was confused and unsure about what to do? Besides, he was the father of a young family.

After I gave the matter a great deal of prayerful thought, a plan began to emerge. I telephoned a highly principled Catholic lawyer who worked at the Detroit Archdiocesan Chancery Office. I had known him since my years with Contact.

In confidence I related the sordid tale, with no mention of the names of the priest or the victim in question. Without hesitation – and to my astonishment – he told me who the priest was. His activities, I was informed, were being monitored because he also worked at the Chancery Office. The lawyer thanked me for the information, and his advice was simple and direct – because of his unbending Catholic principles, Tom Monaghan had many enemies and should be informed as quickly as possible. Time was of the essence. His business, as well as Legatus, could be seriously injured.

I chose to go through the proper chain of command and approached the Executive Director of Legatus. Following that person's seeming initial shock over the chaplain, I was instructed to leave for the day and make a Holy Hour on the way home. The director asked me to speak with no one and said that the matter would be handled personally, promptly and efficiently. I complied with the request, drove to Duns Scotus Chapel in Southfield, made the Holy Hour and went home for the rest of the afternoon and evening.

The following morning, after attending Mass at Legatus headquarters in Ann Arbor and following a proper thanksgiving, I was ushered into the director's office for a closed-door meeting. I was told to immediately pack up all of my personal belongings and leave – my services at Legatus would no longer be required.

Much later, I was informed by a district vice president of Legatus that the director and the chaplain were good friends, to the degree that the chaplain, upon learning that the story of his sexual misconduct was in danger of being brought into the open, insisted that the director terminate me instantly. His orders were carried out and, to all intent and purpose, I was history – or so it seemed.

I had and continue to have enormous respect for Tom Monaghan and fretted over this dilemma of protecting him, the name of Legatus, and the young man who asked me to help him. How could I reach Tom? He was usually protected through a layer of persons who filtered information to him.

During the time I worked for Legatus my admiration and respect for Tom Monaghan grew. His great personal charm is a reflection of his humility, disciplined lifestyle, manly courage and love for God and his Church. I recall the time during a trip to his Drummond Island estate, walking together with him through the woods, singing old familiar Irish ballads at the top of our lungs. Many times the thought has occurred to me – what a great priest Tom would have been!

I set up an appointment with the vice president of Domino's Pizza and, in confidence, recounted the episode to him. He listened intently and promised action. He would get back with me. More than a week passed and there was no response. Thereupon, I wrote Tom Monaghan a letter requesting an appointment, without mention of the reason. Evidently, the letter was received, opened by a secretary and consigned to the wastebasket.

What other recourse did I have? The name Father John Hardon, S.J., came to mind. He had occasionally celebrated Mass at Legatus headquarters, and I found his presence to be riveting. On a few occasions I had briefly spoken with him. At the time he was living at the University of Detroit. It had been many years since I had visited the Jesuit residence there. At one time I had frequently visited Father James McGlynn, my good friend, from the days of Contact.

I arranged a luncheon meeting with Father Hardon. I met him at the residence, and after a short prayer we drove to Proust's Restaurant in Ferndale, just a couple of miles from the University. It's sometimes strange the things we both remember and forget. On that occasion, I recall how Father Hardon enjoyed the rice pudding for dessert. I also recall how sparingly he ate.

Speaking with him was like meeting an old friend. I found no difficulty informing him of my priestly background prior to recounting the sexual advance of the Legatus chaplain toward this young man in the Chicago hotel during the national Legatus conference. He agreed that Tom Monaghan had to be informed. He promised to take care of it and, indeed, he did. It was shortly afterwards that the problems were addressed and the necessary changes occurred.

It was truly the beginning of a great friendship with this remarkable Christ-like priest, but more of that as we proceed.

During my two years with Legatus in Ann Arbor, I became acquainted with Tom Marshall through a couple of his letters to the editor that had appeared in *Crisis*, a monthly Catholic publication. Both letters dealt with the controversial topic of the renewal of the Latin Mass and were extremely well written. Tom lived in Royal Oak, not far from our home, and I phoned him to set up a meeting.

The Latin Mass was the only Mass I had ever celebrated. I mourned its passing! Tom was a leading proponent for obtaining permission to have the Tridentine, also known as the "Classical" or "1962 Indult Latin Rite," Mass celebrated again in the Archdiocese of Detroit. Bishops were allowed to grant such permission but, thus far, none had been given to any Detroit parish. Father Shanaghan was the administrator of St. Joseph's Church in downtown Detroit. He was a devout, holy priest who celebrated the new *Novus Ordo* Latin Mass every Sunday. It was also his wish to celebrate the old Latin Mass and he gave Tom his permission to proceed in seeking authorization from the bishop.

You may well ask: Why was I involved with this group who desired to have the old Latin Mass re-established? My interest in and love for the traditional Mass stems from a number of reasons. I have a deep and abiding reverence for the only form of Mass I ever celebrated, since I left the holy priesthood prior to the wholesale changes that occurred beginning in the second half of the 1960s. The changes occurred not because of *Sacrosanctum Concilium*, the document on the Sacred Liturgy that emerged from Vatican Council II. The changes were due to the *Concilium*, or committee, that was appointed to study this document and to recommend possible improvements in the celebration of the Mass. Archbishop Annibal Bugnini, who headed up the committee, was, unknown to Pope Paul VI, a closet progressive who simply forged ahead on his own. The ailing pope realized too late the damage that had taken place. By then, though, the horse was out of the barn.

Latin is the official language of the universal Church; it is much better suited for both philosophy and theology than are our modern day languages. Missals (Mass books) in my day contained both Latin and vernacular translations that allowed even novices to follow. Now some forty years later, when we observe and compare the differences between the dioceses that allow the traditional Latin Mass with those that do not, those that allow the Latin Mass consistently reap these blessings:

- Beauty, awe and respect for liturgical details
- The emphasis on the sacrificial part of the Mass, its source and summit, that occurs through the double consecrations of the bread and the wine into the Body, Blood, Soul and Divinity of Jesus Christ
- A significantly larger number of priests ordained from those dioceses that have permitted the generous application of the old Latin Mass
- he faithful who attend these Masses have a greater sense of the sacred, of reverence and engaged participation
- Young people who are attracted to the old Latin Mass where the sacred ceremonies help them to discern a religious vocation
- Those who attend these Masses bring the awe they experience back into their homes, and the Mass becomes a part of their lives
- The sacred music of Gregorian Chant fills their souls as do the beautiful hymns that have been discarded in other dioceses

In confirmation, see how blessed are the dioceses of Lincoln, Nebraska, and even such Bible-belt bastions as Chattanooga, Tennessee, Atlanta, Georgia, Tyler, Texas, Little Rock, Arkansas and Taylor, South Carolina.

* * * *

To return to the narrative, four of us Latin Mass advocates took up strategic positions at the various church entrances on two successive Sundays after all Masses. The four were Tom Marshall, Ed Wolfrum, his wife, Sue, and I.

St. Joseph's Church is a magnificent old church lovingly built by a host of deeply religious German Catholics who had settled in that area in the 1920s and '30s. A hushed reverence pervades one's soul upon entering its sacred portals. The altar immediately captures the eye. The dark wood, masterfully carved by gifted artisans, fills the heart with a deep sense of peace.

God tested us that first Sunday morning with a loving gift of heavy rain, but we remained undaunted at our posts. The following Sunday God rewarded us with bright sunshine. All in all, we gathered over 1,500 signatures on a petition to Edmund Cardinal Szoka to grant the Latin Mass to Father Shanaghan's faithful parishioners.

Tom Marshall pulled out all the stops in composing his letter to the Cardinal, who now resides in the Vatican, overseeing the finances of that little state. Then we waited for the results. We waited further, but with growing concern. Finally, a letter arrived. Permission was refused. There was to be no Tridentine Mass allowed anywhere in the Detroit Archdiocese for the foreseeable future.

About a week later Tom received another letter. It came unsigned, and we could only surmise that it was from an anonymous sympathetic member of the Priests' Senate for the Archdiocese. The contents of the envelope contained the actual confidential deliberations of this august group.

In essence, the Minutes of their meeting stated that we were a group out to cause trouble, that we had a hidden agenda, although the report neglected to specify what it was. The letter also stated that if we continued to cause the Archdiocese trouble, they (the Senate) would enlist the members of the Stephen's Ministry [sic], who would soon put us in our place. How odd! The Stephen Ministry's function is to focus on offering aid and support to people in need, while the Priests' Senate is solely to act in an advisory capacity to the Cardinal Archbishop.

How unmanly, how spineless, how ridiculous! We had never met them; they had never met us. It indicated to me how far the character of some priests had fallen since my seminary days.

Later we learned that our petition to restore the old Latin Mass in only one parish in the entire Archdiocese had been pigeonholed. Apparently it never reached the desk of Cardinal Szoka. Fifteen years later, there continued to be no Tridentine Latin Mass celebrated in the whole Detroit district. Only recently, permission was granted to celebrate this Latin Mass in two parishes.

TWELVE

Smelling the Roses

Set your mind on things above,
Not on earthly things.
  Colossians 3:2

I was beginning to feel a bit like the *Man of La Mancha* – tilting at windmills. Again, retirement, for the third time, looked most inviting. We decided we would make a clean break by moving away from the greater Detroit area. Even the moon looked attractive! We opted to move back to Jenison, west of Grand Rapids, where we had settled nearly twenty years ago.

It was 1992. We bade farewell to our friends and drove to western Michigan on what was an unseasonably sunny, warm February morning. We took it as a favorable sign of God's providence. By nightfall we were in our new home and "all-in" because of the physical work. Since neither Ruth nor I had outside commitments, we were able to take our time to make our dwelling livable. (Ruth still feels that our home is not livable!)

It proved to be an enjoyable, relaxed time in our lives. Wonder of wonders, we actually took time out to venture into ballroom dancing classes.

Meanwhile, our two sons continued their education. David earned a Masters' in Information Security. He's now married with two children, living in Virginia on the outskirts of Washington, D.C. Meanwhile, Patrick's art courses at the Center for Creative Studies in Detroit prepared him to do graphic design and illustration for the entertainment industry in Los

Angeles. The nest was now empty. It became a time of adjustment for Ruth and me; time to relax and renew old friendships.

In my search for a parish in the area, I learned that the pre-Vatican II Latin Tridentine Mass was celebrated once a month at Our Lady of Sorrows. I began attending Mass there regularly while Ruth, not yet a Catholic, attended occasionally. It was then that I met a personable, scholarly, orthodox priest – Father Dennis Morrow. He regularly rode his bicycle around the parish and used a city bus in his travels into downtown Grand Rapids. How refreshing! Father Morrow also worked in the Marriage Tribunal office at diocesan headquarters. He holds a Licentiate in Canon Law from Rome and reviews and adjudicates requests for annulments – an unenviable position.

One Sunday we attended Sacred Heart Parish, a beautiful old church in a largely Polish section of the city. We were happily surprised to meet Father Edward Hankiewicz, a warm, upbeat, jovial pastor deeply dedicated to his sacramental priesthood. To our amazement, he also worked in the Marriage Tribunal office with Father Morrow, and he, too, holds a degree in Canon Law. Considering the reputation that lawyers of any stripe have to live down in our society, I regarded my favorable disposition to one canon lawyer a stretch – but two? I could only conclude that the age of miracles was still upon us! Father Hankiewicz's day begins with an hour of prayer before the Blessed Sacrament. Interestingly, his parishioners are also warm and welcoming.

There is something in me that, as the saying states, just can't seem to leave well enough alone. "Why not," I thought, "attempt to obtain permission for the weekly celebration for the old Latin Mass at Our Lady of Sorrows?" To this day it is the Mass that contains a deep sense of the sacred.

Tom Grego, a fearless parish member, had been trying for years to accomplish this task. Together, we approached Father Morrow. His cooperation came immediately and enthusiastically. The plan was simple and direct. He would write Bishop Robert Rose, who headed an eleven-county West Michigan diocese; and I would do likewise.

From the pulpit Father Morrow announced that a petition

for the weekly celebration of the Latin Mass would be taken up for two consecutive Sundays at all Masses. Everything went smoothly. Some were so enthusiastic that they wanted to sign the petition a second time.

Our Lady of Sorrows was a small working-class parish with a heavy concentration of Italians. We were delighted to get 550 signatures for submission to the bishop. The entire package was duly delivered by hand to the Chancery Office. Father Morrow made certain that it reached its proper destination and would not be pigeonholed.

We waited for a response. And we waited . . .

Some months later, I drafted a second letter in which I came straight to the point. I wanted a "Yes or No" answer, with no further delay. It was close to Easter when Father Morrow and I received a reply from Bishop Rose. Permission granted. And so the Latin Mass has continued to the present day, even though the venue has changed to Sacred Heart Parish.

I have been amazed at the large number of young people who attend the old Latin Mass. The sense of the sacred is still discernible, and all of the faithful are attentive and prayerful, as are the priests who take turns celebrating this Mass. The celebrants uniformly observe the rubrics (directives) in the celebration of this ancient ritual, regularly referred to as "the Mass that will not die."

It was during the Latin Mass phase of my activities in Grand Rapids that I began working with Ed Wolfrum. Ed had been one of the famous four "troublemakers" that had collected the 1,500 signatures for a Latin Mass at the beautiful St. Joseph's Church in Detroit.

Ed is a sound production expert who had won a Grammy Award for the reproduction of Lionel Hampton's original melodies. For a reason that I can't recall, I needed his expert service. He made a deal with me. In exchange for his help, I would introduce him to Father John Hardon. Soon thereafter Ed and I arrived promptly on this saintly Jesuit's doorstep. While we were waiting to meet him, I engaged the switchboard operator in conversation. Her admiration for Father Hardon was boundless. She informed me that he received more telephone

calls, local, national and worldwide, than all the other Jesuits at
the University combined.

An assistant led us to Father Hardon's office, which was
downstairs and in the basement of the residence building. I
mean *basement* in its drabbest, gray sense. The décor was "prison
pallor" – cinder block or poured cement walls, floors covered
with worn carpet. The lighting was dim; the reception area
might well be called "creepy," with its well-worn desk, two hard
chairs and a ratty-looking "easy" chair. Some few yards distant,
a single lighted room was adjacent to the secretary/reception
area. Thus, we were introduced to Father Hardon's palatial surroundings.

He rose quickly from his chair to greet us, attired in his tat-
tered Jesuit cassock, a large smile on his face and a twinkle in his
eyes.

Amid the clutter of paperwork on his desk, I noticed a very
inelegant, workaday type old telephone. The room looked like a
joke in a lumber camp. Was this the office that his Jesuit confreres had assigned to him, I wondered, many who had been his
students? Again, there came to mind the nagging thought of two
Catholic churches steadily moving away from each other: The
American Catholic Church and the Roman Catholic Church; the
one progressive, the other orthodox.

There was not a doubt in the world as to which one Father
Hardon gave his undivided allegiance. And there was no doubt
as to which of these wielded the power!

The purpose of our meeting was to obtain permission to professionally redo, as a labor of love, some of Father Hardon's
audiotapes. Father Hardon had produced nine albums of audio
reproductions that included *The Spiritual Exercises of St. Ignatius
of Loyola*, *Angels and Demons*, *The Blessed Sacrament*, *The Profession
of the Roman Catholic Faith*, *Catholic Sexual Morality*, *The Ten
Commandments* and two series on *The Truth Crusade*. Similar to St.
Thomas Aquinas, the topics that he covered both enlighten and
humble the minds of brilliant people; but at the same time are
clear and revealing for simple, faithful souls.

Each album is, in fact, a full semester graduate-level course.
If there were one weak area in the original productions, it was

the lack of professional electronic expertise. Ed had listened to some of them and determined they needed his professional touch. The rest is history. Ed, who had become captivated by Father Hardon within a half-an-hour, wound up re-doing all the audio tapes – nine albums of twelve tapes each. Now they are clear, noise-free transmissions produced by a highly professional sound engineer; and this, even with Father Hardon's soft, ethereal voice. As a bonus, Sue, in tandem with her husband's work, set about illustrating each of the album covers.

It was the beginning of a beautiful friendship. Later Ed presented Father Hardon with a gift of new computers. It was a joy to have been a minor player in this transaction.

THIRTEEN

On the Road Again:
Bishops and Bombshells

Do your best to present yourself to God as one approved,
a workman who does not need to be ashamed
and who correctly handles the word of truth.
　　　II Timothy 2:15

Within three months we were well settled into our Jenison home, attempting to make the adjustment to a more serene lifestyle. As usual, though, answering a phone call was about to change that. Bill Cooke was on the line. Legatus in Toronto had limped to a halt since the events leading to my dismissal. He had called a meeting of the members, who were eager to revitalize their chapter. Would I be willing to work for them, rather than for Legatus, on the basis of a two-year contract and be responsible for their chapter activities? It would require a week of my time each month and my flying to Toronto to tie up the loose ends and revitalize their chapter.

It was an offer I couldn't refuse, and it proved amazingly easy to re-establish the chapter. To cement the relationship with Ann Arbor, Deacon Dan Foley, a charter member of that group, and Terry Coles were invited as our first guest speakers. Our well-respected original spiritual director, Father Thomas Waites, had been assigned a new parish out of the area and a replacement was needed. Bill Cooke had someone in mind – Father Ronald Mercier, a young Jesuit who had recently obtained his doctorate in social ethics. Talk about a square peg in a square hole! It was a marriage made in heaven for us. His name was submitted for approval to headquarters and, hearing no more, he assumed the position with the permission of his Jesuit superior and was with us for two years.

He quickly earned the respect and admiration of the entire membership. On the few occasions he was unavailable, we had Father Dudley Cleary of Opus Dei, a most fervent priest, for Confessions, Mass and spiritual direction.

During this period I was able to line up a list of outstanding speakers from both Canada and the United States. Topics ranged from Canadian industrial development, the state of the Archdiocese of Toronto, the influence on culture of the secular and religious media, social ethics, the impact of the newly published *Catechism of the Catholic Church*, abortion, the growing New Age movement and radical feminism – just to name a few topics. The litmus test I applied to gauge the success of a meeting was to observe how long it continued after it was formally gaveled to a conclusion. There were no speedy exits of business executives. In many cases, we had to blink the lights to remind them it was time to break up.

Our membership prospered both in numbers and in their understanding and appreciation of their faith. Further, the members became more aware of their responsibilities as leaders in their local communities. Quietly they began to offer their many talents to their parish priests, local school boards and community movers and shakers, dedicating themselves as leaven to enhance the culture in danger of descending into paganism.

Over time the tendency to change from getters to givers had measurable impact on the growth of their businesses as well as the well being of their employees. A number of the members, in fact, invited me to spend the night in their homes to further explore some of the issues that surfaced at the monthly meetings.

I recall one such youthful member who worked as an investment counselor and financial planner. At each meeting he became increasingly more enthusiastic as he questioned and pondered the challenging business ethics that were offered. It was a few years later that he made a life-changing decision to put these principles to the test. Along with a partner a new business was initiated with a radical departure from the former business-as-usual format. Over the years I lost track of him until one day, during a telephone conversation with Bill Cooke, I inquired about Kevin. Bill chuckled and replied, "He took off like a rocket. Their new company was and continues to be unbelievably profitable while genuinely serving others."

Now that the Toronto Legatus was up and running again, once a month, on a Monday morning, rain or shine, cold or warm, I was up early in Jenison for a quick breakfast before traveling to the meetings. Ruth would drive me to the Grand Rapids International Airport for the 6:00 A.M. flight to Detroit and then on to Toronto. From there I would catch a bus into town and a taxi to St. Basil's Church, where a room in the priests' residence continued to be available to me. I would participate in the well-attended Mass in the beautiful old church and afterwards walk to Bill Cooke's office. The whole routine was so efficient that I would usually be in my office before any of the other employees arrived at 9:00 A.M.

It was, indeed, a labor of love, from which I derived great enjoyment and satisfaction. Telephone calls came in with increasing frequency on a multitude of questions. The topics ranged from theology to dealing with teen-aged offspring. Even business-related advice was sought.

There was one area where I met with total failure – trying to persuade the Toronto archbishop to support our solidly Roman Catholic chapter and to speak at one of our sessions. He refused every offer. Even my attempt to recruit an official diocesan representative as a Legatus member met with refusal. The archbishop balked at the idea of giving us any official recognition. Why, I'll never understand!

Toward the end of my two-year contract, while all was proceeding smoothly, we were informed that a new chaplain based at the Ann Arbor headquarters would arrive for a visit. He was a convert from the Anglican faith, born in England, a well-known "celebrity" priest. There was no need to meet him at the airport; arrangements had been made to have a lay member of

Opus Dei meet him. There was one favor he had requested – a private meeting with Archbishop Aloysius Ambrozic. This was surprisingly easy to arrange – due, no doubt, to this priest's public status.

Following his meeting with the archbishop, the visiting chaplain arrived at our office. Board members of the Toronto chapter took time off from their busy schedules to greet him. We were told that his meeting with the archbishop had been a purely private and confidential one, with a single exception – the choice of a chaplain for our local Toronto chapter. The Ann Arbor chaplain's choice was a local religious order priest. Our chapter members were dumbfounded! We already had a chaplain whose name and curriculum vitae had been submitted for approval according to the by-laws. Nevertheless, the chaplain from Ann Arbor was adamant: "The Archbishop of Toronto approved my choice." It was his take-it-or-leave-it reply! It was the first and only time that the archbishop had ever formally acknowledged our presence. Strange how he involved himself in this matter when he had no idea, apparently, what we were all about! It is interesting to note that, at one time, the religious order priest selected by the Ann Arbor chaplain to be the chaplain of the Toronto chapter for Legatus had been already approached by two lay members of Opus Dei. Due to his busy schedule, he declined the offer.

Keep in mind, the resident chaplain, Father Ronald Mercier, had the enthusiastic approval of the entire Legatus membership. Our Toronto chapter's board members were beginning to feel like a bunch of Canadian colonials being visited by an imperial English personage. Since that time, whenever this celebrity priest appears on television, feelings of distaste and disgust surface – the phrase "pompous ass" keeps repeating itself and causes me to turn him off.

The Ann Arbor chaplain left the meeting with the archbishop's order intact – my way, or else! Luckily, he didn't hear the comments about his character after he departed from the meeting. They were blunt, pithy, pungent and to the point.

Later, I asked permission to meet with the newly designated chaplain, who administered a private center for university students. Perhaps, I foolishly thought, a compromise could be reached by using alternate chaplains to fill the slot. The next afternoon I took a streetcar that dropped me off only a few blocks away from his quarters. I was shown to his upstairs office to await his return. Upon his arrival, I related the story of the visit of the Ann Arbor chaplain, and he listened quietly to the joint-chaplain proposal.

"Dave," I said, "What are your sentiments?"

"My name is not 'Dave' to you," he responded. "It's 'Father.' You are not a priest, you're an ex-priest!"

I had met this type before, so I let it slide. I was tempted to correct his theology by reminding him that priesthood is forever, but thought, what's the use.

In spite of his busy schedule, the Opus Dei priest consented to meet with the Toronto board members of Legatus. A week later the meeting took place. Unfortunately, Dave – oops, Father – was always deadly serious, while our board members had a delightful effervescence. He sat there mostly silent, uttering one-sentence responses to the questions asked by the board members. (This I do not have from personal knowledge because I was not present. Various members shared this unsolicited information with me.)

In vain, our board members tried to keep the young, personable Jesuit, Father Mercier, as their official chaplain. The arrogant national chaplain again refused the members' request.

When my two-year contract came to an end, I closed the books on this chapter of my life. Soon afterwards, the Toronto chapter just seemed to drift away. On the few occasions when I have spoken with Bill Cooke, he has always continued to be cordial and gracious – a real man's man.

What is the point of sharing this negative narrative, you might well ask? It points, I believe, to the abusive power of one man imposing his will and running rough shod over the protestations of a group of sincere Catholic businessmen who had a real sense of making progress through adopting solid spiritual standards, especially in their treatment of their employees. To this day, the members of this chapter have never regrouped. What a tragic loss to Catholic Christendom!

FOURTEEN

Struggle for Survival

A man's reputation is only what men think him to be;
His character is what God knows him to be.
The Catholic Reader - Anonymous

My life was not serene. Settling into a domestic routine proved more difficult for me than anticipated. Nagging – even guilty – sentiments that I should be "doing something" kept intruding on my peace of mind. What good was all my reading, writing and studying if the Good News was not being imparted, shared and discussed with others? On Sunday mornings over several months, Ruth and I visited well over twenty churches in search of a genuine Roman Catholic parish, apart from the one where the Latin Mass was celebrated. As mentioned previously, that, too, had been moved from Our Lady of Sorrows to Sacred Heart of Jesus Parish. The Mass at 12:30 P.M. was inconvenient. Also, Ruth, continuing to struggle with Catholic practices and attitudes since Vatican II, found the Latin Mass difficult to understand, appreciate and follow.

No schism in the Catholic Church had been publicly declared; but, in all truth, it had occurred. An ever-widening gap continued between the Roman Catholic Church and what has come to be known as the American Catholic Church. Over time official teachings were either put into practice with increasing reluctance or simply ignored. The Church of Rome was seen as coming from a Neanderthal age that attempted to impede social progress. The cry was and continues to be: Shed your medieval tenets, drop your antiquated dictums and take a step into the modern world. Paraphrasing Gilbert Keith Chesterton, the brilliant journalist, poet and defender of the faith, "The Church's traditions and teachings had not been tried and found wanting; they were found too demanding for our secular, pleasure-seeking culture and not been tried."

Rarely was anything mentioned from the lectern about dress or decorum. Coveralls, shorts, revealing tops, and short skirts were all increasingly more evident. Even if something were said, was there expectation of any change? Was there authority behind the words? And even if something were said, the same attire appeared Sunday after Sunday. Imperceptibly, the guidance of the priest came to have little or no effect on many in the congregation. Also increasingly evident was the conspicuous absence of men at Sunday Mass. While Catholic men were once a force to be reckoned with, women in ever-increasing numbers were taking over as lectors, cantors, servers and so-called extraordinary Eucharistic ministers. Indulging the whims and inclinations of the faithful seemed the prime focus of parish life.

Why was this happening? If anyone had deliberately set out to destroy the Roman Catholic faith, they could not have invented a better means of doing so. But, you ask, who is to blame? Look no further than the bishops of the dioceses. The buck stops here!

The Church can never do its job by consulting opinion polls. Bishops cannot let the Pope take the heat while they sit back unwilling to address unpopular teachings and practices. It is cowardice, betrayal, and abdication of the responsibility of the sacred offices of bishop. The problems assailing the Catholic Church today are what they have always been in any of the Church's ages. Look no further than weak episcopal leadership. This, too, has caused the dearth of vocations to the priesthood. It also explains why the second largest "denomination" in the United States today, after Catholics, is *inactive* Catholics who rarely, if ever, see the inside of a Catholic church.

In the midst of this Catholic confusion and frustration, Ruth decided to join the local Bible Study Fellowship group. I felt very encouraged by her newfound passion for her group – more than

500 women gathering weekly to pray, sing hymns of praise, discuss and apply Biblical passages. My attention was thoroughly grasped by this interdenominational program, founded in 1960 by a missionary woman from China, A. Wetherell Johnson. One Sunday after church services in San Francisco, when Johnson had returned from the Far East, she was asked by five women to develop a Bible study program for them. Her program quickly spread across the United States and has now become international.

By no means is this an easy course! Those dedicated souls who pursue it spend many hours researching the Scriptures and then write how this or that particular section of the Bible impacts their own daily lives. It's a challenging course, but few drop out. Its leaders are well prepared; each week they must spend considerable time in prayer and study in order to do justice to the program. Their dedication is reflected in the fact that they faithfully telephone at least sixteen small-group participants each week. During the eight years in which Ruth participated, I can count on one hand the weeks that these leaders missed calling her. Shirley Walker was one of Ruth's discussion leaders and they became dear friends. Shirley has consistently proven her great love for God, family and friends.

Ruth pursued her own agenda. She felt affronted and sickened by the treatment she had received over the years from members of the Catholic Church. Through Bible Study Fellowship she determined to prove that my religious convictions were in error and to try to persuade me to join some non-Catholic Christian denomination. Often she has, tongue-in-cheek, threatened to have me buried from a Protestant Church if I neglected to treat her well.

At the time of her joining the Bible Study Fellowship, the group was reflecting on the words and meaning of Saint Matthew's Gospel. A year later, while studying the Book of Exodus, the focus included the story of Moses leading the Chosen People through the desert. The specifications set down by God for worship in the Tabernacle during their 40-year sojourn captured her special interest. The ceremonials, the instruments of worship, the vestments – all were thoroughly scrutinized. Gradually, Ruth came to recognize this as the pre-cursor of the Sacrifice of the Mass. Later, during a lecture by Father Joseph Fessio, S.J., she learned that Gregorian chant, encouraged and used by the Roman Catholic Church over the centuries, had originated 600 years prior to the advent of Christianity in the Temple worship. It was the chant used in the singing of the Psalms in those ancient days.

She was beginning to come full circle in her study of the Church's doctrines and practices. Her continued association with Bible Study Fellowship armed her with a barrage of ques-tions for me, leading her ever closer to Roman Catholicism. In spite of all the Catholics over the centuries who had given scan-dal, including even a few popes, she finally understood that this was the Church that Jesus Christ established.

She continued her association with her Bible Study "groupies," as I jokingly called them, and today we rarely go out in public when someone from her classes doesn't stop her with a friendly greeting. Their kindness and caring is truly inspiring, and I have come to realize how much genuine Christian love they have in their hearts. Many times I reflect on the reasons why so many of our Catholic people have joined one of these truly loving denominations. In doing so, they have deserted not *Roman* Catholicism but *American* Catholicism.

An example: Dick and Shirley Walker daily attempt to live their faith to the hilt. The former Dean of Students at Grace Bible College, he had been the successful owner and operator of two thriving franchises, appropriately named Heavenly Ham. They have five grown children and twelve grandchildren (so far). Both parents, interestingly, have dedicated their lives to be exemplary grandparents. They devised, among other things, a "Cousins Camp," a concept that can be easily replicated. It's a one-week summer get-together of tightly structured activities for grandchildren over the age of five. How the children look forward to living with "Grammie and Grampie!" Each day begins and ends with prayer, while during the day there is a steady sprinkling of Bible quizzes and religious instruction. The greater part of the day is spent on recreational pursuits – swim-ming, horseback riding, ice and in-line skating, visiting children's museums, and many other activities. Would that more mature couples spend their time, talents and treasures on such fulfilling apostolates! The time invested with their grandchildren throughout the year is reflected in the youngsters' cohesiveness with the extended family.

The Walkers had invited us to dinner one Thanksgiving. Following a delicious repast, I addressed what I thought was a simple question to one of their daughters, "Dawn, what are your thoughts about your father?" She did not take the question lightly. "No one has ever before asked me that question," she replied. "He has always been here for all of us, and I'm afraid I have taken him for granted."

Our conversation was interrupted, and I thought no more about it. Two weeks later I received an e-mail from this forty-year-old mother of two, and it begs to be shared in its entirety:

I'm not too quick on my feet. Your question about my father was so loaded and so full of emotion for me that I'm afraid I didn't communicate exactly all I wanted to say. I lay in bed last night for quite a while trying to boil it down to a brief essence. Here's my try –

Both of my parents model and have modeled, as long as I can remember, hard work, fierce loyalty, honesty, unbelievable faithfulness to those they love and programs they are dedicated to, and a love for God. As long as I can remember they have prayed with me and for me as well as for my siblings, each other and for those they love. Every morning before we went our separate ways, God's Word was read, discussed and made practical for our day and the challenges we faced. Often before nighttime prayers, they would apologize for hasty or harsh punishments or just plain wrong judgment. They are not perfect. They are the first to admit it, and I know them too well to claim that, but they made a commitment as a young couple to give themselves and their family to God. It is not in an attempted perfection or even the human efforts for that matter, but the openness to letting God be the leader. I know a lot of good people . . . hard working, loyal, honest, faithful, dedicated people to great causes, but without salvation through Jesus Christ as the center and Jesus Christ at the helm, their good deeds are only that, instead of multiplied exponentially and eternally as my grandmas', great aunts' and parents' have and continue to be. The secret recipe is not in the people but in their God.

Jeremiah 9:23–24 says, "This is what the Lord declares: 'Let not the wise man boast of his riches, but let him who boasts boast about this: that he understands and knows Me, that I am the Lord, who exercises kindness, justice and righteousness on earth, for in these I delight,' declares the Lord."

As I watch my parents agonizing over our loss this year, I also see their trust in a very real and present God. That is what I most admire about them. Because of that love and devotion, and its outworking in their lives, when I read about a loving, compassionate heavenly Father and the beautiful family of God, I can believe it because my parents have given me a glimpse of what God has graciously prepared for me for eternity!

I home school not because I am the cleverest and most creative but it is my desire, my deepest desire, to have the maximum amount of time and exposure with my children to pass along this heritage. This is the pearl of great price, to know God, and to have passed and continue to pass His love and reality to me, Tom, and now my children, as well as every person they have the privilege to meet.

Let's fast-forward to July 16, 2001. That was the day when Ruth was operated on for breast cancer. Shirley Walker was at the hospital with us at 5:30 A.M. for Ruth's first operation. At noontime Dick appeared on the scene with a Heavenly Ham box lunch. Prior to Ruth's second operation, on August 27th, Dick and Shirley were again present and brought along two mutual friends, Sam and Becky Vinton. Sam had been a missionary in Africa. As a pastor, Sam used this occasion to offer a special heartfelt prayer for Ruth's full recovery.

By comparison, in neither of my wife's surgeries, even though it was requested in this Catholic hospital, no priest at any time appeared on the scene – neither before nor after. Is it any surprise that so many of our former Catholics have drifted away to be received with loving respect into the arms of such Christians!

Do I have an unreasonable vendetta against bishops? To answer, let me recount a couple of personal happenings in this Grand Rapids Diocese. Through a casual conversation with a solid, orthodox Roman Catholic professor at Aquinas College, I was informed that their enrollment was down in 1994. This information caused me to do some follow-up investigation.

It happened that a young man of my acquaintance had abruptly left Aquinas to study elsewhere. His sudden departure resulted from his first day in a religious education class. He told me that the Dominican sister teaching a course on the Blessed Sacrament began with the following statement, "At the outset, I want all of you to understand that I do not believe that Jesus is present in the Eucharist." My young friend immediately picked up his books and left.

I telephoned three priests who professed and practiced authentic Catholicity. Their comments to my question, "What is your impression of Aquinas College?" elicited these responses: "It's not Catholic." "I wouldn't send my dog there." And the third one, "If a student wished to preserve his faith, I would choose Calvin College over Aquinas every time."

These interchanges resulted in my meeting with the president of Aquinas, Paul Nelson, with whom I shared my findings. It was refreshing to learn that he greatly desired to see the college return to its roots. He further asked if I would develop a statement for presentation to the college's Board of Directors.

Following the old Packard Motor Company motto – "Ask the man who owns one," I contacted the Franciscan University in Steubenville, Ohio, and asked for Father Michael Scanlan, who was president at that time. I had met Father Scanlan through Legatus. Franciscan University had been a party school by reputation. Through persistent effort, it took Father Scanlan fourteen years to turn it around to a truly Catholic college. He returned my call that afternoon. Briefly I filled him in. Then, for most of half an hour, I listened and took notes. Without missing a beat, he instructed me from his own experience on what was required to turn Aquinas around.

My second call – made the following morning – was to Christendom College in Front Royal, Virginia. Christendom is a jewel of a small college nestled in the Shenandoah Valley. I asked for the president, Dr. Timothy O'Donnell. He reinforced the advice of Father Scanlan, adding sage observations as I furiously scribbled away.

My third and final call was to Father Leonard Kennedy, a Canadian Basilian priest/friend, scholar and builder of educational facilities. He responded to my request for help. "I have just what you need," he said. "I'll put a package in the mail for you today." Three or four days later it arrived from Canada. The old saying is still true: "If you want something done, ask a busy man to do it."

It was relatively simple to put a statement (see Appendix) together for Aquinas College. My summary, along with the supporting documents, was completed on May 19, 1994. It focused on those responsible for the proper coordination of the facility – the Board, finance, administration, public relations, faculty and students. Even now, as I re-read it, it gives the impression of a comprehensive, no-nonsense document – no thanks to me.

When I completed it, I immediately presented it to Paul Nelson. I even took a risk by telling Paul that I was quite ready to take whatever flak might be coming my way, especially from any of the Aquinas professors. I had nothing to lose and everything to gain. Besides, who ever heard of a shanty Irishman running away from a good fight?

Paul duly presented the six-page plan to the board members. It received a thorough review and a decision was quickly reached – a compromise in their eyes. After all, they agreed, we already are a Catholic college and therefore have no need for change. Case closed!

When the local bishop at that time was asked about Aquinas, without hesitation he responded, "It, indeed, is a Catholic institution of higher learning."

American Catholic, perhaps, but not Roman Catholic!

I was saddened to learn – from a sincere, devout priest – that the same bishop had made a statement to the effect that he wished he had never given permission to allow the Latin Mass in his diocese. Each week more than 150 faithful regularly attend that Mass and help to financially support this inner-city parish. Also, there are six to eight priests who regularly volunteer their services to celebrate this Mass where the sense of the sacred is so obvious.

Why this negative attitude on the part of the bishop?

A growing number of Catholics, faithful to the teachings of the Roman Catholic Church, attend Mass at parishes other than their own – and sometimes with devastating consequences. Such was the case with Ray and Susan Grabinski. They live and home school their children on a 30-acre parcel of land. Their oldest son, still at home – a bright, mature lad for his age – had only started to baby-sit. On Pentecost Sunday, when the younger children were ill, in order to minimize their time away from home, the parents attended Mass at the local church in Greenvill8e for the first time. The Grabinski family ordinarily attended the old Latin Mass at Sacred Heart in Grand Rapids, some forty miles distant from their home.

At Communion they both approached the altar and Sue with her infant daughter, Ann Marie, in her arms, knelt so that the priest – the parish priest, in this instance – could place the Host directly upon her tongue. (The custom is allowed and so stated in the Church's official directives.) The priest ordered her to stand to receive. Sue politely informed him that it was their custom to receive their Lord on their knees. Upon hearing this, Ray immediately moved forward and knelt next to Sue on her left. The priest attempted to bypass both of them, but Ray on his knees shifted over to kneel in front of him. This time Ray explained to the celebrant that they always received on their knees. The priest became angry. Holding the sacred species in his consecrated fingers, he threatened Ray with the words, "If you don't shut up and leave, I'm going to call the police." He further told them that unless they did as he directed, he would refuse them Communion. The Grabinskis held their postures.

By this time, Sue, clutching her infant daughter close to her, was in tears. Callously, the pastor summoned the ushers to remove them – forcefully, if necessary – from the church. Ray, not wishing to cause further grief to his wife, rose, helped Sue to her feet and, surrounded by ushers, left the church. Both had been refused Communion! As they reached the outer door, the parish priest declared to the congregation in a loud voice, "This is what right-wing troublemakers do." Some parishioners applauded his remarks; others were horrified at the pastor's scandalous behavior.

Ray, no shrinking violet, promptly wrote the bishop, seeking redress for the injustice. The bishop, who appears unable to handle confrontation, never replied. Letter after letter have gone into the bishop's office from Roman Catholics concerned over a great number of abuses. Their concerns have no impact, and nothing is heard further. Evil, in no way, tolerates truth or goodness. Rather, it not only tolerates but also actually encourages mediocrity.

I once wrote this bishop a personal and confidential letter requesting a meeting with him to discuss my concern over inactive priests hiring themselves out around the diocese to celebrate Mass and allow pastors the opportunity to "take time off." This practice, as every bishop knows, is strictly forbidden. My letter and the envelope bore "PERSONAL AND CONFIDENTIAL" clearly visible on both. I received a response, not by letter but by telephone, not from the bishop but from his vicar general. He informed me that the demanding schedule of the bishop was such that it would be perhaps months before a meeting might be arranged. In turn, I informed the vicar that inasmuch as the letter and its contents were for the bishop's eyes only, confidentiality had been breached.

My confidence in the bishop dwindled and had all but disappeared.

The bishop finally took early retirement. The usual age is seventy-five. It was his wish to be given the right to appoint his own successor. Petitions had been sent to the Vatican from both priests and laity asking Rome to appoint a bishop of its own choice. We prayed for a manly bishop, faithful to his high office, a sacramental bishop, a pastoral bishop, a teaching bishop; one who will reflect our Lord in all ways in his own life. We prayed for a bishop who belonged to the Roman Catholic Church rather than to the American Catholic Church. We prayed for a man such as Bishop Kevin Britt, whose time with us was precious, important and all too short. We should continue to pray also for our recently retired bishop as he prepares himself for his ultimate final journey.

FIFTEEN

Catholic Courses and Cautious Clerics

Preach the Word; be prepared in season and out of season; correct, rebuke and encourage – with great patience and careful instruction. For the time will come when men will not put up with sound doctrine. Instead, to suit their own desires, they will gather around them a great number of teachers to say what their itching ears want to hear. They will turn their ears away from the truth and turn aside to myths. But you, keep your head in all situations, endure hardship, do the work of an evangelist, discharge all the duties of your ministry.
   II Timothy 4:2–5

The success of structured non-denominational Bible Study Fellowship courses intrigued me. In today's materialistic culture the ability of our local group to capture and sustain the interest of 500 women (one of 982 similar groups internationally with class enrollment of 150 to over 500) is truly remarkable. Completion of the course requires a seven-year commitment and many personal home-study hours each week. As Ruth gradually continued toward a deeper understanding and appreciation of authentic Catholicism, her convictions progressively influenced her written answers to the questions in the weekly discussion group.

   The women in her small group noticed her responses in class and became curious about her different perceptions. She was simply adding a Roman Catholic dimension to the discussions. Often discussion continued over lunch to further explore religious truths from a more Catholic tradition. Rarely was Ruth home immediately after classes concluded. I also noticed that our incoming telephone calls had increased. Over the years, I had come to admire these truly Christian women who openly professed their personal relationship with Jesus. Often, when I'd answer the phone, before handing it over to Ruth, I'd tease them unabashedly. (Remember, we tend to tease only those we like!)

All of these things were happening as I was in the midst of pondering a similar course that reflected legitimate Catholic practice and doctrine. Search as I might, I was unable to find a satisfactory course anywhere in the diocese. What I had in mind was something both attractive and challenging, offering truth and goodness for the mind and the will – soul food.

Here was one of the many problems besetting me. From 1966 to 1995, one-and-a-half generations (a generation is usually considered twenty years) of Catholics had been fed a steady diet of progressive mush and pabulum. Thus, logic dictated that I reach back into pre-Vatican II days for a proper place to start. One champion whose name immediately came to mind was Archbishop Sheen. Providentially, right at that very time a series of his videocassettes was being advertised in Catholic periodicals. Ruth, with her usual womanly intuition, quietly purchased them for me as a Christmas gift. They proved ideally suited to my purpose. The archbishop's talks, covering an assortment of intriguing topics, splendidly contrast the Church's formulated beliefs before the Second Vatican Council with the misleading reformulated direction after the Council.

The Second Vatican Council bulks as a watershed in the modern history of the Church. The term "pre-Vatican II Catholic" has come to imply someone of another age and almost another religion. It is invoked to contrast a person unfavorably with one who believes that he is adhering to what Vatican II actually teaches. Those making such a contrast need to pay more scrupulous attention to the actual teachings of Vatican II.

Incredibly, after forty years the *Conciliar* documents have yet to be implemented. Why not? It is because of the progressive persons who seized power and consistently dissented from the truth in conformity with their wayward lifestyles. Those who glibly speak of the "spirit" of Vatican II have deliberately, and so far successfully, blocked out what the official Church attempts to teach.

To return to the teaching course that I was pondering, Ruth and I offered Bishop Sheen's videos with modest beginnings on Ash Wednesday evening at Sts. Peter and Paul's Parish Center in inner city Grand Rapids, attracting more than seventy-five attendees from two parishes. We continued with meetings on successive Wednesday evenings when the group assembled to absorb the inspiring video messages. Stepping up the level of discourse, I presented our students with thought-provoking questions based on Archbishop Sheen's videos; questions designed to spur deeper reflection and more profound discussion.

The questions were designed to provoke thought but not unduly so as to frustrate or discourage. Thus, especially during the beginning, classes were often punctuated with long periods of silence. This was necessary to encourage dialogue. The current generation of Catholics had not been taught to come up with proper answers to tough questions. However, the group's initial reticence in responding gradually faded until we found ourselves going over the two-hour time limit. We adjusted to the situation by officially ending on time, then taking an extra hour for those wishing to informally pursue a more in-depth appreciation of the articles of our faith.

The structure proved to be soul satisfying! Father Dennis Morrow, the pastor, was an occasional visitor, a generous supporter and an enthusiastic participant. He is solidly Roman Catholic and I consider him one of the brightest priests in the diocese.

During the summer months and a long-delayed fall vacation to Europe for our 30th wedding anniversary, the courses were put on hold. When we resumed, I made an error in judgment and accepted an offer to relocate our study group to an affluent suburban church activity center. It had everything we needed, and was even closer to where we were living. The acoustics were great; the electronic components for video viewing were first-class, state-of-the-art. The seats were new and comfortable rather than cold metal, with well-arranged tables for convenient note taking and discussion. With most of the same enthusiastic crowd behind us while picking up a few others in the process, we invaded the 'burbs.

The videos we chose to present at our new location came from a Call to Holiness conference in Sterling Heights, a northern Detroit suburb.

Call to Holiness, the brainchild of three outstanding priests, was conceived in an attempt to counteract the influence of Call to Action – an organization placing individual conscience and personal experience above what the Roman Catholic Church actually teaches.

Regrettably, an improperly informed conscience can easily lead an offspring of Adam's fallen nature down any number of destructive blind alleys. Similarly, attempting to develop a set of principles based on our myriad life experiences is impossible and leads in turn to selfishness. It's like the man who jumped on his horse and rode off in all directions.

With such an emphasis on experience, it is no accident that the "me generation" came into being. Already a part of the American cultural scene, Call to Action, which originated in Detroit in 1976 and went on to spawn some 200 similar groups, gave it further impetus. Call to Holiness, unfortunately, was twenty years late in getting out of the gate in November 1996. Only now is it beginning to form chapters in the United States; it has four while Call to Action has forty.

Word soon circulated about the videos we planned to present in the "hallowed" halls of St. Pius X's Parish Center, resulting in even greater numbers in attendance. The first video featured Father Robert Sirico, the founder and director of the Acton Institute, a conservative think tank that quickly gained national prominence. The title of his talk was *Prudence and Politics; Sanctity and Action*. It was a no-nonsense presentation laced with humor and anecdotes from Father Sirico's own life.

He refers to himself as a "revert" – he was born a Catholic, left the Church and returned after fourteen years. He was ordained a Paulist Father and assigned to the Grand Rapids Catholic Information Center. Unbending in his Roman Catholicism, he became a source of concern and embarrassment to other Paulists. They regarded him as an indictment of their progressive lifestyle, a blot on their escutcheon. Finally, they encouraged him to leave. He has since founded an order of Oratorians in Kalamazoo, Michigan.

Father Sirico's video message was not the pabulum and drivel usually presented in parishes. It triggered more than a little uneasiness in the power group of the St. Pius X administrative staff. They decided to give us a second chance; perhaps the first video had been an aberration. Surely, the next one would be more palatable. Two weeks later, the video star was Dr. Timothy O'Donnell, President of Christendom College in Front Royal, Virginia. His topic was *The Laity and the Church Militant*. To the horror and consternation of the ruling authority at St. Pius X, Dr. O'Donnell took over where Father Sirico had left off. In no uncertain terms he addressed the need for a militant laity. It was too much for the parish power brokers and we were history!

The St. Pius X pastor, the late Monsignor John Nadowski – he was also dean of the diocesan clergy – had permitted us the use of the hall. He was on vacation at the time we got our marching orders. We were told that the parish center had suddenly been taken over by different parish groups. Returning from vacation, Monsignor Nadowski was informed of our forced departure. With a stern look on his face he promised to get to the reason for our dismissal. Due no doubt to his busy and important schedule, he never got back to me.

Reflecting on the entire incident, I feel it was a manufactured excuse (a blatant lie). I was further disillusioned by the caliber of our so-called Catholic leaders, both clerical and laity. Again, I was not surprised in view of the many rejections I had experienced. Quite frankly, I had come to expect this type of behavior and attitude from the majority who profess to be Catholic. They believe in being tolerant of anything or anybody except for those who profess to be obedient, loyal and steadfast to the Roman Catholic Church. Discouragement flooded my heart whenever these rejections took place, not so much for myself, but for those who were eager to learn and maintain their faith.

Our little study group was starting to feel like a tribe of nomads wandering from one oasis to another. There were so few inviting parishes!

I contacted Father Hankiewicz of Sacred Heart of Jesus Parish located in the inner city – in my book "one of the good guys wearing a white hat." Actually, he wears a black biretta, an official liturgical headgear for approaching the altar for Mass, a custom that has almost vanished over the years. With not a moment's hesitation he offered his church basement for our video series. But the nomadic lifestyle caused severe attrition in our numbers, and we dwindled to thirty or so faithful followers when Fr. Hankiewicz welcomed us to Sacred Heart's basement. Providentially, the parish had just received a gift of a video projector from a successful businessman.

By this time I was beginning to feel like a surfer in search of the perfect wave. How could we raise the bar, preserve the interest and vitality of our group and escalate this challenge?

I recall two Jesuit retreats that I had made during my seminary years. Both were right out of the *Spiritual Exercises of St. Ignatius*, founder of the Jesuit order. In the first retreat, the spiritual director was totally blind and well advanced in age. We found ourselves in awe of this saintly man. I'll never forget how devoutly he celebrated Mass with wholehearted and reverent concentration. The unchanging prayers he knew by heart. For those prayers earmarked for a particular saint or feast day, he used a Braille altar missal. Two deacons in their final year of study guided him about the altar. The reverence was so hushed at such times. Both his words (all in Latin) and his gestures filled with reverence of God's presence were such that the two hundred seminarians present were in awe of his sanctity.

In the second retreat, two or three years later, our Jesuit retreat master dynamically recounted one instance in his life after another relating to the purpose of the retreat. With good humor, he informed us that after the Scriptures, two great books on the spiritual life were acknowledged supreme: *The Imitation of Christ* by Thomas à Kempis and the *Spiritual Exercises of St. Ignatius of Loyola*. "We Jesuits, in our deep humility," quipped this retreat master, "acknowledge that what the *Spiritual Exercises* contain is only the second greatest spiritual book to be written in the entire history of the world."

In recalling these two seminary events, I decided it was time to introduce our group to the writings of St. Ignatius, who founded the Society of Jesus, the Jesuits. Father Hardon had assembled a series of twenty-four audio recordings, each lasting approximately thirty minutes, based on the *Exercises*. Inspired by the group's dedication, I wrote a summary on the *Spiritual Exercises* aimed at enhancing class participation and designed to be used in conjunction with the album containing the twenty-four talks. Later, I presented a copy of the summary to Father Hardon. I was greatly moved when he approved and blessed it. This further enhanced our wonderful friendship that lasted until the time of his death. Since meeting him, I have never been the same.

We hung in there through twenty-four sessions. Many who attended these audio presentations found the *Spiritual Exercises* to be a genuine spiritual awakening. Until then, they said, they had not really grasped what Pope John XXIII had been trying to tell people when he spoke of *metanoia*. They had not understood that the Greek word does not call them to surface or external alterations. It summons them to transformation in the deepest chasms of the soul, where, with God's help, the beatific dimensions of true happiness here and hereafter are realized.

SIXTEEN

Great Jesuit, Holy Priest

Remember your leaders, who spoke the word of God to you.
Consider the outcome of their way of life and imitate their faith.
Hebrews 13:7

During the course of my journey, three men stand out. All have had a deep influence on my life. Father Bill Lane in Gainesville, Texas, Arvid Jouppi, the Lutheran automotive analyst, and Father John Hardon. Father Hardon had, by far, the most profound effect.

It took the apostles some time to realize that Jesus was the Messiah and the Son of God. Only over time did I come to realize that Father Hardon was recognized as this country's leading Roman Catholic theologian and catechist. More than any other, it was this saintly priest who helped people to come to realize that there were two Catholic Churches in the United States – the American Catholic Church and the Roman Catholic Church. While the American Church sought to develop pseudo-Catholics, Father Hardon was busy spiritually and intellectually equipping the laity to come to a knowledge, love and appreciation of authentic Catholicism. During the turmoil of the last forty years, he was a beacon of light in a storm-tossed sea for thousands of otherwise confused, disoriented Catholics.

A closer association with Father Hardon was enhanced upon presenting him with a copy of the summary of the *Spiritual Exercises of St. Ignatius* that I had developed through listening to his audiotapes. On his fiftieth anniversary to the priesthood, I further presented him with a unique memento.

While on a trip to Europe for our thirtieth wedding anniversary, Ruth and I had stopped in the little town of Friesach in Germany. There, on a side street on top of a small incline, was a beautiful Gothic church. The tour guide casually mentioned that St. Thomas Aquinas, the great Doctor of the Church, had preached from its pulpit.

In his own day, St. Thomas was famous for simplifying doctrine for the unlettered common people so that they could understand and appreciate their faith. Father Hardon had this same ability. At that time in his life, he was busy simplifying St. Thomas' writings for modern consumption. Throughout Father Hardon's writings, the doctrine is first defined in true Jesuit fashion; then, he takes three paragraphs to tell what each definition means. So simple, so direct, so inspiring and so understandable!

Alone, I began to walk toward the church, a bit of an uphill climb. As I reached the front of the church something strange occurred. I faced a very large, round, black door opener with the words practically engraved on it, "Please turn me and I'll open the door for you." I grasped the wheel-like opener with both hands, but I couldn't move it. I tried again several times to budge it but to no avail. Saddened by my failure to enter the church, I meandered along the side of the building toward the altar end, searching for another entrance. Alas, there was none. The church, I decided, was solidly locked. I returned to the front of the church and, exerting extra pressure on it, attempted again to open the door. Still failure! I was deeply disappointed; I so much wanted to see the pulpit from which St. Thomas had spoken to the devout townspeople. What to do?

I left the grounds feeling defeated. I noticed a man in working clothes about to pass by as he walked along the lane adjacent to the church property. I gestured to him. I was in luck; he spoke English. I asked him if he knew how to get into the church. He smiled and said, "Yes, follow me." He approached the door that had been my Waterloo.

Without hesitation he took the door opener in his hands and

with no effort, gently, easily, opened the door for me. "No," he answered me, "I am not the church caretaker; I am just passing by." With a smile he departed as I thanked him.

Inside, the church was dark and not another person present, except our Lord. After offering up a prayer at the communion rail, I located the ornate pulpit near the left transept. Looking up, I imagined St. Thomas standing there inspiring the faithful with his simple words of wisdom. My never-to-be-forgotten time spent in that church lasted no more than fifteen minutes. As I left, the door closed quietly and firmly behind me. How often I have thought – I should have tried that church door one more time. In all truth, it would have yielded easily, I am quite certain. And, yet . . . It was then that I heard the horn of the tour bus announcing its departure. It was a five-minute jog for me – just enough time to climb aboard.

At the time of Father Hardon's fiftieth anniversary to the priesthood, I handed Father Hardon the memento – a photograph of the church that Ruth had taken – I recounted the entire story to him. I noted a slight glistening in his eyes as he took it in his hands and reverently kissed it. He was profuse in his thanks for such a thoughtful and precious treasure. I had the sense that he and St. Thomas Aquinas had been good friends for a long time.

During his lifetime, Father Hardon wrote more than forty books. One of these, *Catholic Catechism: A Contemporary Catechism of the Catholic Church*, has sold over a million copies and is still going strong. It paved the way for the monumental, long-expected and fervently desired *Catechism of the Catholic Church*. He acted as a consultant for that catechism as well. In the midst of his writing, he found time to record a dozen sets of messages on every imaginable topic. Each set is a jewel in itself! The series on angels fascinates many people. It includes a lesson on the presence of Satan in the lives of men that brings with it a sobering reality. I bring this up since I have felt the hot breath of the evil one on my neck many times.

Each day Father Hardon spent an hour in prayer before the Blessed Sacrament and, like Archbishop Sheen, did most of his writing on his knees. Someone, who knew him well, estimated that from the time he became a Jesuit he spent 50,000 hours on his knees in the chapel.

I am embarrassed to recount that, after our relationship deepened (he had a great and droll sense of humor) and I would receive a phone call from him, I'd ask if he were still a Jesuit – or had his Jesuit confreres converted him. I tried to make light of the rejection he received from his Jesuit brother-priests, many of whom he had taught. It was one of his great sorrows. Not the fact of being rejected, but of their turning away from their great traditions and joining the ranks of the American Catholic Church. The much admired and beloved "iron men" Jesuits of yesteryear have greatly diminished. I pray God for their return!

Recently, a nationally prominent Catholic educator suggested that all Jesuit universities throughout the country should be closed because, he claimed, none was Catholic today. My own brother Vincent, also a Jesuit, now in his eighty-eighth year and living in a Jesuit retirement home, rarely, if ever, attends the gatherings of his Jesuit order. Experience has taught him to avoid such spiritually empty meetings. My brother, by the way – and I say this not because he is my brother – is as close to Father Hardon as any priest I have known: poverty, chastity and obedience along with humility and loyalty to the Holy Father; like Father Hardon, a real man in the true sense of the word.

Father Hardon's father died when young John was a year old. Later, when he searched for a father figure, he found it at John Carroll University, which was run by Jesuit priests. There were certain strengths about the Jesuits in those days, a manliness that he had never before experienced. Their mental discipline also was a large factor in attracting him into their ranks. Already an outstanding scholar, their powerful mindset inspired him to major in philosophy and shape his virile approach to spirituality. Similarly, St. Ignatius had been a soldier who shaped the *Spiritual Exercises* along military-discipline lines. What a tragedy that many of today's Jesuits have either abandoned the exercises or changed their focus until the courage and resolve of manliness has all but disappeared.

In 1994 Ruth and I completed Father Hardon's *Advanced Catechism Course*. It is a series of thirty-six lessons ranging from approximately forty to one hundred and eighty statements (depending upon the topic) which have to be answered either true or false, plus other interesting figurations to stretch one's intellectual prowess. Should you choose to challenge yourself with this course, or even with his basic course, make sure to say a fervent prayer to the Holy Spirit before starting. I assure you, these will challenge your ingenuity!

As of this writing, I am teaching this course to eighteen stalwart Catholics – no other adequate word to use. One adult student who had completed her Master's degree stated, "Getting through this is more difficult than graduate school."

At the time when Ruth and I undertook this course, Father Hardon asked me if I would also critique it for him; so I did. Too often my frustration bleeds through in my critiques. The interesting thing is this: The group now taking this course – two lessons away from completion – never miss answering the questions. They faithfully attend the sessions and challenge many answers until they learn what Father Hardon tries so diligently to impart. The students even take the time to mail their completed lessons for correction when they are ill or out of town.

For the novice student, a *Basic Catechism* course is now offered. It is now a requirement to complete it before venturing to the advanced course. Again, not easy by any means! Thus far, ninety catechists have graduated from the basic course, and now eighteen stalwarts from the advanced. They know their faith and will make prime teachers of Catholicism today. Thus, the genius of Father John A. Hardon!

During the years that Father Hardon had known Ruth, he would gently ask, "Ruth, when are you planning on becoming a Catholic?" He suggested February during one of our conversations. As the years slipped by, he often repeated the question. One evening Ruth quipped, "Father, you never said what year!" Without flinching, he turned to her and said, "Never mind February. What about this year – in March!" He finally wore her down.

On March 24th, 1996 at a beautiful and reverent ceremony in the chapel at Assumption Grotto in Detroit, Ruth entered the Catholic Church. Afterwards, we renewed our marriage vows before God. Benediction was a perfect ending. Later, during the Easter season, the Sacrament of Confirmation was bestowed upon Ruth in Grand Rapids.

This great Jesuit was not interested only in Catholics. He applied himself in understanding Protestantism, and in 1956 published *Protestant Churches in America*; still considered a standard text in Protestant colleges today. His teaching skills were sought by a number of Protestant seminaries and colleges as a visiting professor. He never refused these offers. Interestingly, they wanted him to teach Catholic theology, fully aware that what he offered was not watered-down mush but uncompromisingly Catholic.

Keep in mind that he was doing this long before Vatican II encouraged ecumenical dialogue. Among other places he taught was Bethany School of Theology, Lutheran School of Theology and Seabury-Western Divinity School where, for the first time in history, a Jesuit was allowed to participate.

Many of Father Hardon's sayings continue to be remembered:

"Nothing happens by accident, nothing happens by chance!"

"We must always look to God's Providence to understand whatever comes into your life. Accept it, submit to it and put your total trust in God's plan for you. Whatever He sends to you is for your sanctification and salvation."

"Call them by their right name; not dissenters, but heretics."

"Whenever a progressive theologian or priest engages you in conversation and begins attacking the Church in any way, your first statement should be: 'Tell me about your lifestyle.'"

Father Hardon would remind married couples that their home was a domestic church where they, as parents, bestowed God's grace on each other and on their children every day. He never stopped reminding parents to daily bless their children. He never let me forget that I was still a priest with responsibilities to carry out. Whenever he called for help with some project, he would address me as "Father." At the end of our informative conversations, he would say, "Now, Father, before I hang up, I'll give you my blessing in Latin. You give me yours afterwards in English." The next time he would say, "Whose turn is it to give the blessing in Latin?" And so we would switch the language each time.

Each of Father Hardon's days was filled with prayer and work. He was advisor to at least two popes, Paul VI and John Paul II. He was Mother Teresa's spiritual advisor. He regularly gave retreats to the Missionaries of Charity throughout the world and taught them theology. Thousands of people sought him out for help, both physical and spiritual. No one was turned away. Amazingly, at a time when Confessions are so disregarded, he went to Confession daily, to obtain all the graces he could in order to sustain himself. As he grew older, he fought cancer, asthma, a heart defect and approaching blindness, accepting them as gifts from God. He lived what he preached!

Several times in these pages, I have written of the rejections I experienced after my defection from the priesthood. How small and insignificant they are in light of this beloved, faithful man of God. When he celebrated his fiftieth year in the priesthood, an event which Ruth and I attended, there was not a single other Jesuit present.

The priest/editor-in-chief of the *Michigan Catholic* would not allow Father Hardon's picture ever to appear in that paper, and his name could only be used in the smallest type possible. When asked about this treatment, the editor simply replied, "He's divisive." How could he be divisive if he only taught authentic Roman Catholicism handed down for centuries? How well Father Hardon sought to imitate his own rejected Lord.

Father Hardon died of bone cancer on December 30, 2000, at age eighty-six. Eternal rest grant unto him, O Lord, and let perpetual light shine upon him! May his soul and the souls of all the faithful departed rest in peace.

*   *   *   *

One of Father Hardon's many legacies is a short piece: *A Prophetic Warning*. It is especially relevant at this time of confusion and division within the Church.

I believe the breakdown of religious life in the Western world is a phenomenon that is unique in the history of Christianity. There have been, since the last half of this century, more departures from Catholicism, more closing of Catholic churches, more dioceses that have been secularized than ever before in the history of Christianity. We are living in the most deeply de-Catholicized age of Christianity.

The United States has been one of the main victims. In general we may say the more academically educated, the more wealthy and the richer in this world's goods a nation was, the greater has been the departure from Jesus Christ. Only God knows what the future will be, but judging by the last five hundred years, there has been a far-reaching breakdown of authentic Christianity . . .

In the Catholic Church we have seen the most widespread breakdown of the priesthood and authentic consecrated life. In my thirty-third year of working for the Holy See – just a few things I can share with you. The Holy See seriously wonders how much of the Catholic Church will survive in wealthy prosperous nations of the Western world like our own. What then is the remedy? There is only one way that the revolution can be reversed – and it had better be reversed. Professed Catholics who call themselves Christians must reexamine their faith. We must be sure we believe that God became man in the Person of Jesus Christ. We must believe that when God became man He instituted the Holy Eucharist. We must believe that the consecrated life – of consecrated poverty, consecrated chastity, constant obedience is most pleasing to Jesus Christ. When God became man, He made sure He lived a life, I repeat, of consecrated chastity, obedience and poverty. What I want to share with you is that, not only religious life, but the Catholic Church will be preserved only where there are – hear it – Catholics who are living martyrs, do you hear me?

Ordinary Catholics will not survive this revolution. They must be Catholics who are thoroughly convinced that God became Man in the person of Jesus. They must be convinced there is only one supreme authority on earth: the authority of Jesus Christ vested in the Vicar of Christ. What the Church needs, desperately needs, are strong-believing Catholics. Otherwise, one nation after another, like our own, will be wiped out as a Christian country.

In a remarkably short time after his death, Father John Hardon's cause for beatification was initiated by Edward

Cardinal Gagnon who resides in Rome and who worked closely with Father Hardon. It will come as no surprise to his close friends if he is proclaimed a saint; and, then, recognized as a Doctor of the Church. In the 2,000-year history of the Roman Catholic Church, only thirty-three saints have had this honor bestowed upon them. Since the Church moves slowly and cautiously, it is impossible to know when these events may occur.

SEVENTEEN

Holiness Comes To Call:
Detroit Strikes Back!

There is no conflict between the old and the new;
The conflict is between the false and the true.
The Catholic Reader – Anonymous

How to expand Father Hardon's course materials in similar fashion to that of Bible Study Fellowship still kept rumbling around in my mind. Surely we could match the success of Bible Study Fellowship, I thought initially. Then, it occurred to me that cultural standards had significantly deteriorated since the 1960s, when Bible Study Fellowship had begun expanding. At least, I temporized, we can make a beginning.

Call to Holiness, the already-mentioned theologically ortho-dox Roman Catholic movement, had recently been formed in the Detroit area. Its leaders proceeded to initiate gatherings of faith-ful members of the Roman Catholic Church to counteract the influence of Call to Action, also meeting on the same weekend in downtown Detroit. Call to Holiness sets aside a weekend every fall during which devout, faithful Roman Catholics are reinvig-orated and edified by celebrated Catholic speakers. These gath-erings attract 1,800 to 2,200 brave souls. The question I kept ask-ing myself – What support do they, a minority, have throughout the rest of the year? Do they simply languish until the autumn of the following year and then become revitalized?

I felt that it was crucially important to develop support

groups that would assemble every two weeks. Using Father Hardon's basic course in Catholic doctrine and practice, I felt that it was not only doable; it was necessary. Ruth and I, determined to use our first-hand experience, spent the summer assembling a comprehensive booklet. With everything but the kitchen sink in it, we had a complete "how-to," paint-by-numbers guide to set up Call to Holiness chapters nationally.

Three priests took the helm in founding the annual Call to Holiness conferences. One of them was Father Eduard Perrone, pastor of Assumption Grotto Church in Detroit. Father Perrone sought to counteract the inroads of Call to Action that had planned a large convention in Detroit in the fall of 1996. He then solicited the assistance of two theologically orthodox stalwarts. It should come as no surprise that he went to Father John Hardon, who had a working office in the Grotto parish. Father Perrone's plea for assistance was hardly out of his mouth when Father Hardon replied, "Let's do it." A quick phone call to Mother Angelica, who put together the international television studio, Eternal Word Television Network, (EWTN) elicited her instant response – she would be honored to be the keynote speaker at the first convention.

Jesuit Father Joseph Fessio, founder and editor of Ignatius Press, was the third helmsman. Informed of the parish intent, he said: "No, no, that won't do. Let's think big, state-wide, with a number of prominent speakers." And so Call to Holiness was born. Every year since, the three-day weekend conventions have gone from one success to another.

*   *   *   *

There is another dimension to Father Fessio not as well realized. He founded the St. Ignatius Institute within the Jesuit-managed University of San Francisco. Like most (if not all) colleges and universities controlled by the Jesuits today, USF is decidedly progressive and oriented towards the American Catholic Church. Through its well-respected Great Books curriculum, faithful to authentic Catholicism, the Institute was established to counteract the university's liberal/progressive bias. Although the Institute enrolled only two percent of the student body at USF, this percentage included many of the university's brightest and best. Time after time they took home top academic honors. This became an embarrassment and a frustration both to administration and faculty of the University of San Francisco who had dumbed down academic standards across the rest of the campus.

What to do? In January 2001, Father Stephen Privett, a fellow Jesuit, took the reins as the university's new president. In short order, he fired the two administrators of the St. Ignatius Institute; changed its name to Catholic Studies Program while removing its unique focus. Can you imagine any academic worth his salt eliminating such authors from centuries past as Homer, Plato, Aristotle, St. Augustine, Dante and St. Thomas Aquinas; or modern writers in the ranks of Tolstoy, Dostoyevski, Herman Melville and John Henry Cardinal Newman?

Beaten down, bowed, bloodied; yet undaunted, Father Fessio and the fired administrators, along with three of the Institute's key faculty members, founded Campion College. It has two campuses, one in San Francisco, the other in Washington, D.C., each independent of other institutes of higher learning. Each started with fifteen students. When St. Ignatius Institute surfaced as Campion College, USF released a statement. "Campion is not accredited." Campion countered with a list of its accreditations by Michigan's Ave Maria College, Franciscan University of Steubenville, Ohio, and the International Theological Institute in Gaming, Austria.

The empire struck back through Father Thomas Smolich, Father Fessio's Jesuit supervisor. On May 11, 2002, he ordered Father Fessio, one of the most respected voices of traditional Catholicism in the United States, to break off all ties with the fledgling Campion College. He was even forbidden to contact Campion. Then, this faithful son of St. Ignatius of Loyola was summarily dispatched (read "exiled") to serve as assistant chaplain at a southern California hospital.

Before striking out nationally with Call to Holiness, there was one overlooked detail that Father Hardon brought to my attention. We discussed it privately. How would an inactive priest (me) be perceived heading up a Call to Holiness national chapter-development program? My favorite Jesuit promised to phone me within three days. He called back in two. He had contacted a cardinal working in the Vatican but would not divulge his name, at the Cardinal's request. (I'm ninety-nine percent sure who it was.) Permission had been obtained for me to proceed!

Phyllis Bausano, Father Perrone's secretary at Assumption Grotto, who had gone to Rome for the beatification of Padre Pio, took the chapter development materials Ruth and I had prepared. She presented them to two cardinals who gave it their blessing and approval. I thought, "It doesn't get much better than this!" Was pride beginning to raise its ugly head?

Meanwhile, back in Michigan, as the deer-hunting season of 1999 opened, we made our first official presentation during the annual Call to Holiness conference, with 1,800 faithful Catholics present.

Unfortunately, only a perfunctory announcement from the dais invited those interested in forming chapters to attend a meeting at 7:00 P.M. Only sixteen from that large group showed up. I shrugged off the disappointment, thinking: "So, we'll go with quality rather than quantity." The step-by-step materials were handed out along with a number of supporting documents. It was a no-lose plan. Father John Hardon's catechetical expertise was handed on a platter to this group of elite Roman Catholics, along with instructions on presenting the program in their home territories. In this manner, implementation would be unified throughout the country rather than haphazardly. I thought, "If it worked so well for Bible Study Fellowship, it could also have a similar degree of seeing the light of day in our wounded Catholic culture." Apparently, I did not realize just how wounded our Catholic culture was, or how deeply the wound had penetrated!

The sixteen potential leaders left the meeting on a positive, enthusiastic note. Yes, they would put in the required time and effort to prepare themselves for this much needed apostolate. Finally, I thought, chapter development had moved from inertia to action. We were on our way!

On January 10, 2000, almost two-and-a-half months since the initial gathering in Detroit, our sixteen volunteer leaders were contacted by surface mail, reminding them that it was time to begin. A second letter was duly dispatched to fourteen other potential leaders requesting a reply by February 21st. Only one woman responded. Many times I have since wondered why the lack of response. Was it apathy? Yes! Was it lack of interest? Yes! Was it lack of zeal? Yes! Often, we hear it stated by sincere Catholics, "Don't worry, the battle is already won," as if that absolves us from any effort in the process. Under such circumstances, that attitude becomes presumption. Is it because, twenty-five-plus years later, we have been beaten down and marginalized so many times by the American Catholic Church which, since 1967, has seized and maintained the diocesan seats of power?

Many years ago, I recall an astute, articulate priest visiting from Scotland making the observation: "You American Catholics will move heaven and earth to save a soul but you won't move a little finger to sanctify one." Where did the truth lie?

Gradually, I heard back from a few of those present at the November chapter development meeting. Each had a legitimate reason for non-action – or so it seemed. Then slowly, almost without effort, some chapters began to form. Two years later in 2002, there were four chapters – not an encouraging number . . .

In discussing this whole episode with a young astute Christian Reformed gentleman I deeply respect and admire, he responded with wisdom, "People don't follow programs, they follow leaders!" Facetiously, I have advised this young man to search for a devout young lady to knock the remaining small rough spots off him. He looked at me with a wry eye, as if wondering about my sanity.

*   *   *   *

Returning to the year 1998 . . .

During my conversations with Father Hardon, he often asked me about inactive priests. He was most concerned that those who might wish to return to active pastorates be able to do so under appropriate ground rules. I put my ideas on this subject down on paper for him, and he began to formulate an approach to make this happen. At the Call to Holiness conference in 1998, attended by a surprisingly large number of priests, he called a separate special meeting for them to attend. Father

Hardon asked me to brief them on the inactive-priest situation and the desire of some wanting to return. I was gratified at the interest of these good men. Some actually remained after the meeting for further discussion.

It was not until the following summer that I made progress in this specific area of concern. Much of the delay was due to Father Hardon's failing health. In consequence, he deputized a parish priest to take over the task. I learned of a seminary apparently specializing in aiding priests who had left and wished to return. The priest deputized by Father Hardon, a good, holy man whose name I will not divulge, decided that a retreat might be the place to start. I was dubious about attending, since he planned to gear the retreat to active priests only. Nevertheless, I did as he asked me. I contacted all the priests who had been present at our initial meeting and arranged for them to attend a three-day retreat. I cleared my own schedule, but to my surprise and disappointment, no invitation arrived for me. "Inactive priests need not attend," I thought.

Later, upon more mature consideration, it occurred to me that, even today, many active priests really don't know yet how to relate to us. And, I realize that it will take even more time and thought to determine how best to bring some of us home.

Following Father Hardon's death on December 30, 2000, a bishop, perceived as theologically "orthodox," assumed the role of directing the catechetical series developed by Father Hardon. I sent this bishop two letters dealing with chapter development and received no response. I sent him a third letter on July 23, 2001. This time I poured out my heart to him, writing at 1:30 in the morning, when sleep escaped me. I asked him not only for study courses; I pleaded for his counsel in assisting inactive priests wishing to return to their Father's home. How might they be encouraged and supported? And how might I be involved in the process?

No response from him. As bishops go, so goes the Church!

Whenever I feel sorry for myself or feel life is cruel, Ruth and I visit Steve Feldpausch. His smile of greeting fills my soul with joy. Steve has seven young children, ages three to thirteen. A champion wrestler in high school, he has a degree in engineering. A few years ago his physician told him that he had Lou Gehrig's disease, which carries a grim prognosis.

We visit him at Metropolitan Hospital, where he is confined to either bed or wheelchair, almost totally paralyzed. Steve can only move the muscles around his eyes and his mouth. Over many months he labored many hours composing letters to each of his children. Steve's twin Michael, also an engineer, devised a special computer hook-up through which Steve is able to communicate. This system allows Steve to operate a computer using the muscles of a single eyebrow. He types one laborious letter after another. His children are to read them only when they reach their sixteenth birthdays. Each letter contains marvelous advice and encouragement on how to conduct their lives with courage and according to Christian standards.

It is my fond hope that sometime these letters will be published for the edification of many families. Rarely have I experienced such courage as I have seen in this incapacitated young man. He has indeed been an inspiration since the day we first met him.

One day while we were visiting Steve, Ruth wholeheartedly expressed her gratitude for his prayers and example, when her spirits were flagging at the time of her cancer treatments. Whenever I leave his room, I give him my blessing and pray with him and, then, I bend over and put my brow on his arm, asking him to bless me.

Steve did not come by his strong faith accidentally. His mother and father, Jeanne and Barry, are the Catholic counterparts to our Protestant friends, Shirley and Dick Walker.

In my efforts to be a leaven in the Catholic community over the years, I have received some minor degree of assistance and encouragement from the institutional Catholic Church. But, mostly, I have encountered indifference, rejection, arrogance and a catalog of other responses not in keeping with Christianity.

How do I keep going? My association with this brave, delightful young man has been a constant source of strength to me. We all need a Steve Feldpausch in our lives to remind us of an old saying: "I cried because I had no shoes, until I met a man who had no feet."

EIGHTEEN

Let Your Voice Be Heard

And this is love: that we walk in obedience to his commands.
II John 1:6

In February 2002, I received a telephone call from my old Trappist friend who had left his order to marry. It had been years since we had communicated. His call informed me of a reunion, a social gathering of "former" priests, previous religious men and women, and seminarians. The spouses of those who were married were also invited. Mark urged me to attend this event, scheduled to take place on Saturday, March 23rd at St. John's Center for Youth and Family in Plymouth, Michigan. It took no prodding! St. John's Center was formerly St. John's Provincial Seminary, teeming with vocations until the mid-1960s.

I decided to develop a questionnaire from which I made thirty copies – surely there would be no more than that number who would attend the event. When Ruth and I arrived, we were astounded to find over two hundred people present. They came from all parts of the country. Many of the priests we had worked with through Contact were absent; those present at this gathering, for the most part, had left the active ranks of the priesthood sometime later.

We were an aging group, to be sure. Observing us, no one could have said that this was a group of priests. Basic black and a Roman collar do not make a priest, but certainly help. Appetizers, beverages and dinner were served buffet-style allowing the participants sufficient time for socializing. With the help of one interested inactive priest, now a general construction contractor ready to retire, we distributed all thirty copies of the questionnaire. He knew most of the priests present and chose to have them handed out to those whom he judged most likely to respond. One month later only nine inactive priests had replied. The questionnaires contained a significant variety of responses. The following is a list of the questions asked and the replies received.

When did I leave the active priesthood? The answers varied from 1964 to 1999, with most of them leaving between 1968 and 1972.

Why did I leave the active priesthood? Five indicated that it was to marry. Another answer said, "entered for the wrong reasons," but did not specify what they were. Another stated that he refused to live his priesthood according to diocesan directives. [Surely, he must have been aware of what those directives were before he was ordained.] A third stated, "I didn't leave the Church, the Church left me" – without further explanation as to how such a turn-around occurred.

What became the source of my livelihood? Teaching, counseling, family therapy and psychology dominated. One indicated that he had repaired all of the electrical problems in a monastery. Upon leaving he became a master electrician and formed his own electrical contracting firm. In the process, since he was not interested in riches, he gave away almost everything he had earned. Another person started in construction and ultimately became a general building contractor with a thriving business.

Why do priests openly criticize the institutional Church and continue to remain within its ranks and enjoy its support? There were different answers. For instance, there are always those who like to "gripe" in attempting to justify their own actions. Some simply enjoy the priestly lifestyle as well as the honor of being called "Father," but dislike the discipline the Church imposes on them. Some remain in its ranks due to a sense of security while looking for institutional changes when a married clergy would be permitted. [They will have a long wait. Indeed.]

Why don't certain bishops rein in certain priests? The

answers ranged from the following: Bishops would suffer for taking a strong position. They lack courage and fear to alienate priests due to the shortage of priestly vocations. Many of our lay people who have become American Catholics favor the ideas that dissident priests promote, and bishops are afraid of facing the anger of these people if they rein in the dissent priests. Many cowardly bishops want to be politically correct, are really fearful and derelict to lead as shepherds of the flock. [Keep in mind these are the answers received from the nine responses.]

If circumstances and opportunity were present for you to be invited back into the ranks of the active priesthood, would you consider such a move? One inactive priest stated, "Even after thirty-five years, if I had the opportunity, I would return." Another indicated that due to the fear of being crucified, as he stated he was as he left the priesthood, he would not consider returning to the active ranks. One wrote that he would return only if the Church would accept a married clergy. It was sad to hear one answer that it was now too late: he was too old to go back. Another answered to the effect that he missed celebrating Mass and that would be the most important factor in drawing him back into the priesthood. Two others answered this question, short and to the point: "Yes," and "Absolutely."

Are you aware of any such movement in the Church structure today? In your opinion would a warm welcome to returning cause a flood or a trickle? None knew of any such movement. [I recently heard of such a center without substantiating the fact – Holy Apostles Seminary in Cromwell, Connecticut that has a program to assist returning priests with their re-entry process. Also, I was informed of hundreds of such requests being petitioned in Rome.] There are mixed answers as to predicting the number who would consider returning. The reasons given are feelings of abandonment by Church officials after they left and they no longer feel they are part of the Church. Some felt that neither the clergy nor the laity would welcome them. A couple indicated there was little need for inactive priests to return because certain pastors invite inactive priests to celebrate Mass on Sundays while the pastor takes a vacation. One telling remark was to the effect that the longer priests remain inactive, the more comfortable they tend to become.

If you were to return, how would priests in the active ministry receive you? Open arms? Hostility? Suspicion? Resentful? Curiosity? Some thought that because of the present shortage both bishops and priests would welcome them with open arms. Only a few would be curious and a very few of the active priests would be hostile towards them. Again, some who stated that priests are not a homogeneous lot and that all of the above sentiments would surface at one time or another.

How would the laity react to the return of a Prodigal Son? Some thought the laity would be curious, welcoming, cautious and well receiving. One indicated that a recent poll showed that 70% of the Catholic laity in "the American Catholic Church" favored a married clergy. [The Holy Father has stated time after time that although celibacy is a discipline of the Church and not a doctrine, there is no intention of this discipline being changed in spite of all the polls and wishful thinking.]

If you return to the active priesthood, how would your lifestyle differ from that of your former lifestyle in the priesthood? Responses included: Much more prayer and fasting, more time spent hearing Confessions. On the opposite end of the spectrum, an inactive priest observed that he would have to work less if he returned and would look forward to enjoying a nice vacation in Florida each winter. A strange answer from one was that he would be less constrained by fear. Again, more prayer, better prepared homilies, more concentration on being a sacramental priest and less time socializing. One answer indicated that he was daydreaming about having a loving wife to come home to in the rectory each evening after a hard day's work.

As a returned priest, what changes would you like to make/see in the structure of today's Church? Less canonical influence in trying to control the lives of the clergy. Utilizing the faithful in running the physical needs of the Church would be the order of the day. [To a great degree, this is already occurring. In a local parish, the former pastor was referred to as "our part-time priest." Only occasionally was he present among the faithful.] A third answer submitted was to allow women to be admitted to the priesthood as well as to decision-making rules. [In the Roman Catholic Church, ordination of women to the priesthood is not allowed according to divine law. This is not a matter of discipline, but a matter of doctrine! Neither this pope nor any pope in the future has the authority to change what has been believed and practiced for all of its history.] Another inactive priest would put the emphasis on the parish as a loving family with the focus on the Blessed Eucharist. Another statement: "I would do all in my power to teach the children of the parish about Jesus and how to imitate Him in their daily lives. Frequent Confession would be encouraged. Since there is such a shortage of priests, I would train altar boys and encourage the young girls to become active as choir members. Receiving the Sacraments of Confession, Holy Communion frequently would be part and parcel of my priestly ministry."

When speaking with a number of the priests present at the reunion, it was my observation that those who blamed the Church for their departure had no desire to return. Those who recognized personal weaknesses and pointed to themselves as the reason for their defection stated they would happily return if circumstances would allow.

In speaking with many of these men, I could sense the hidden hurt and anger over what was felt to be a total lack of interest on the part of many of the clergy for their departed priestly confreres. Unfortunately, many of these men, at least from a human perspective, appear to be irretrievably lost due to bitterness, disappointment and immersion into the secular culture, or to a total lack of interest after many years of being on the outside. Let us never forget that they are priests forever and remember them in our daily prayers.

Several times, I have been asked the question: "If you were suddenly left alone at this time in your life, would you consider returning to the active priesthood, if the Church would permit it?" My usual answer has been, "I'd go back only as a brother in a monastery where I would be assigned the task of cleaning out the stable." The problem with that answer is: Where to find a monastery today that maintains and uses horses or sufficient piles of manure to make the job challenging and interesting?

It would be my effort to take one day at a time – no grandiose plan but rather to daily place myself in God's providential care. I would wish, of course, first and foremost to daily celebrate Mass in a quiet setting. Next would be the recitation of the Divine Office, plus a daily Holy Hour in a chapel. Whatever writing I might be inspired to do would occur at this time in the presence of Our Lord. Keep in mind: We can talk without thinking but we cannot write without thinking. Divine enlightenment is a grace of which I am sorely in need.

The rest of my day would then be spent in the service of my brother priests. It would be a joy to be perceived by them as an understanding and helpful confessor and spiritual director. Confessions would be made available at several convenient hours during the day for priests in a closed, darkened, secured confessional in conformity with availability and anonymity.

Loneliness is a cross that many priests are asked to carry throughout their lives. How to mitigate its difficulties, soften its harshness and console its recipients? The essential element is for each priest to practice a daily Holy Hour in his own parish church. It offers surprising recuperative powers because of the superb company he keeps during that time. If he feels overwhelmed with responsibilities, this daily practice would tend to slow him down and submit his life to a better perspective.

There is yet more positive fallout from this daily practice – somehow, word gets around the parish, and devout people quietly drop in to join him during that period.

During my years at St. Augustine, one day a seminarian from my home parish asked to speak privately with me. I must have been in my second year of theology, while he was a couple of years behind me. He told me that he felt he was on the outside and unable to get in. His early years had been a sheltered, protected life at home and he had not experienced much of the "give and take" aspects of life common in those years. What could I do to help him?

I asked for support from a couple of my classmates and brought him into our activities. Especially through sports, he began to find acceptance. In hockey, he was a washout. However, in tennis and baseball he proved over time to be at least adequate. Introducing him to these activities, plus bringing him into a wider circle of friendly seminarians, helped him to feel accepted. It became noticeable that much of his shyness disappeared and a new level of confidence took its place. How successful were these efforts and his willing cooperation? I am not entirely certain, but he ended up as the Bishop of Hamilton Diocese.

In my first parish assignment in Kitchener, Ontario, I thanked God for the presence of St. Jerome's College, established there since the 1920s. The Resurrectionist fathers, a great teaching order, manned it. Looking for priests with whom to associate in those early days, I would often visit the college. They, in turn, recognizing the fact that I was in a busy parish with an aging pastor, invited me to join them for their regular social get-togethers in the evening. They would gather, usually around 9:00 P.M., for a game of basketball, hockey or touch football. I became a regular enthusiastic participant. Afterwards – a cup of coffee or hot chocolate, and I was off for the night to the rectory. Did it help? By all means! There were absolutely no thoughts of leaving the priesthood.

All priests need to be made aware of their responsibilities towards their brothers in Christ. If a priest notices one of his brothers moving away from the herd, he must immediately, instinctively and lovingly make every attempt with Christ-like gentleness to bring him back into a priestly group setting.

NINETEEN

The Unraveling of the American Church

Do not take advantage of a widow or an orphan.
If you do and they cry out to me, I will certainly hear their cry.
My anger will be aroused . . .
Exodus 22:22–24

During the 1940s, 1950s and early into the 1960s, the Roman Catholic Church in America was fairly bursting at the seams with vitality. Its influence, feared by some, was everywhere recognized. Churches, schools, hospitals, nursing homes, rectories and convents were being built at an unprecedented rate. Top-notch seminaries teemed with vocations to the priesthood; convents with waiting lists of dedicated graduates from high schools and colleges prepared young women to become devout teaching sisters and nurses. On Sunday mornings, churches were filled to capacity with four or five Masses being celebrated. On Saturday afternoons and evenings there were long lines of penitents, each waiting his or her turn to receive an outpouring of graces through the Sacrament of God's great mercy.

In those days Church leaders spoke out with a single, unmistakably clear voice about what constituted goodness and virtue and what were the tools used by the world, the flesh and the devil to lead us down forbidden, sinful paths. There were established objective standards of conduct to be followed, and even though we sometimes or often failed, we tried to observe them with God's help and to get back on our feet every time we fell down.

With great frequency, priests spoke of the respect that all should extend to the workingman and of the dignity and sacredness of the family. This dignity and respect was extended by no means only to Catholics but to all people, regardless of religious beliefs.

Perhaps, I can give a concrete example. During the period we are describing and even earlier, my family lived directly across the street from St. Anne's parish rectory, which accommodated four priests. One of its residents, Father Charles Mascari, was the pastor of the nearby St. Anthony's Italian church. His was a late vocation, with him having worked as a head-purchasing agent for a large department store. Over and above his sacramental duties, he took it upon himself to become a whirlwind of influence to the first generation of Italian immigrants, many who worked as laborers in the local steel plants. He insisted on the best education possible for their children, both boys and girls. The parents were to expect nothing but excellence from their offspring in the pursuit of higher learning.

The results of his zealous efforts can be seen even today. So many Italo-Canadians (the name of the original professional football team in Hamilton) with whom I associated excelled in their studies and achieved influential and professional positions in the community. Whenever I visit my brother and three sisters, I make it a point to at least telephone my buddies of yesteryear. When Father Mascari's name comes into the conversation, as invariably it does, there is such an outpouring of affection for him. Their children and grandchildren continue to reap the benefits of his fatherly interest and his philosophy of "onward and upward."

The pastor of St. Anne's was a recognized leader among men. Father Joseph Englert of German ancestry was a highly revered and beloved pastor. The church doors were unlocked at 6:45 in the morning and closed at 9:00 at night. It was a rare moment when not a single parishioner was present for a period of adoration.

Like clockwork, following an after-school game of baseball or football in the schoolyard, we would drop into church for a quick visit before going home for the evening meal. This was standard procedure for all of us. As always, there he was, the pastor, quietly praying in the left transept under the overhanging light, making his daily holy hour. I can see it now – the light shining on his bald head. He was primarily a sacramental priest, then a pastor and teacher. Was he influential in the local community? If you could go back and ask the many men searching for gainful employment during the Depression and early post-Depression years, they would respond with a heartfelt "Yes." He maintained a listing of these unemployed men and was on the phone daily in contact with the captains of industry, seeking work for his needy parishioners. The then-Bishop McNally stood shoulder to shoulder with him rendering his personal support. Non-Catholic neighbors out of work received the self-same love and consideration as he gave his parishioners.

It would be a decided challenge to discover such a zealous parish today, some fifty-plus years later. The question that comes to mind is: Why?

It was, of course, the advent of Catholicism "lite" – the emergence of the American Catholic Church that surfaced in the later 1960s. The seeds had been sown earlier in preparation for the great change and takeover which occurred. We have already been introduced to some of their leaders, the so-called *periti* or episcopal advisors who accompanied their bishops to Vatican Council II. These were the self-styled, self-serving intellectuals who unduly influenced, intimidated and overwhelmed weak and morally erring bishops. They sold their "sinful and reprehensible lifestyle" bill of goods to weak members of the clergy seeking to change church doctrine and practice to conform to the manner in which they chose to live. Recent history attests to the victory they achieved. Since the 1960s they have never looked back!

The hierarchical Roman Catholic Church has consistently been counter-cultural, striving always to lift up weak, sinful humanity. The democratically oriented American Catholic Church is culturally attuned, merging and sleeping with the world, the flesh and the devil. Thus, its leaders actually contribute to the moral turpitude running rampant in our culture.

Rather than acting as a dam to hold back the polluted waters of the seven deadly sins, they have become conduits of their contamination. Catholicism "lite" is not the answer to acting as a leaven in solving the cultural problems of our generation. The path of genuine reform is for the church leaders, its bishops and its priests to insist that the Church in America return to its true Catholic identity.

I am convinced that the most effective and direct way to bring about the desperately external reform of Catholicism is to begin with the seminaries. From the mid-1960s, whenever they perceived an opportunity, the dissenters from Church doctrine and practice made great use of their intellectual grapevines to trivialize such issues as priestly celibacy and Catholic sexual ethics in these advanced schools of priestly formation. Father John Hardon once remarked that all seminary students since 1962 should be required to repeat their clerical studies. Another intriguing question to ask is this: How many of those ordained since those tragic days have ever cracked a theological textbook? For the most part, the unsuspecting students who entered those venerable halls of learning with minds and hearts filled with goodwill were victims rather than villains. My heart often cries out to those poorly educated priests who were assigned to progressive seminaries. Were their bishops aware of what was happening? If not, why not?

I still vividly recall the vision of the Roman Catholic Church and of its priesthood as taught in my days as a seminary student. This vision was impressed upon us by our priest professors and repeated many times during the seven years of our intense preparation. The vision was this: The Church sees herself as much more than a tightly woven system of religious thought and practice. Rather, she was, is and continues to be, to the end of ages, the conduit given to her in trust by our Savior Himself, to distribute that infinite ocean of supernatural strength which flows from the pierced sacred side of our Redeemer. This ocean flows especially through the seven Sacraments, the fruits of that redemption born on Calvary. They find their way pure and uncontaminated as they have for 2,000 years into the hearts and minds of the faithful – from birth to the end of earthly life. The very essence, then, of a priest is not that of pastor or preacher, however necessary these functions are in his clerical activities. He is primarily sacramental, the dispenser of God's sanctifying grace into his own soul and the souls of the faithful.

Following Vatican Council II, great effort was made to downplay this sacramental character in favor of a pastoral approach. The "new" church became much more this-worldly than otherworldly, resulting in a diminished sense of sin. This, in turn, led to the false belief that all people are saved, which again resulted in people logically concluding that prayer and the practice of virtue were no longer of great importance. Ideas do indeed have consequences, and it is easy to see now how the fuzzy self-serving ideas of the progressive leaders have led us down the garden path – and I do mean down. We now face, if not the worst, certainly one of the worst, crises in the 2,000 years of Catholic history, and there have been crises aplenty – Christianity versus Christendom.

Those espousing Catholicism "lite" caused the current disaster in large part. There is only one solution – a total renunciation of American Catholicism – an undeclared heresy – and a genuine turnabout, *metanoia* (that word again!), as we eagerly embrace authentic Roman Catholicism in the totality of its beliefs and practices. Once again, we listen to those beautiful words of the repentant St. Augustine speaking to us over the years from the fourth century, "You have made us for yourself, O Lord, and our hearts will always be restless until they rest in Thee." Especially do we pray for those errant episcopal leaders to return to the true house of the faith!

The dilemma is this – as a hierarchy we look to our bishops to lead us home. What do we do when the bishops (not all) are part of the problem?

In place of that innocuous horizontal mantra, "peace and justice," which allows for all types of questionable this-worldly social activism, listen to how Mother Teresa explained and lived it. In her own humble and inimitable manner, she breathed life into that phrase and gave it a vertical and horizontal approach. "Prayer begets faith, faith begets love, and love begets service on behalf of the poor."

The American Church with its purely horizontal secular focus is missing out on the power of humility directed vertically. How often today do you see a priest on his knees preparing to celebrate Mass? How often do you see him on his knees making a Thanksgiving after Mass? How often do you see him reading and praying his Divine Office? A significant number of young people today, realizing that they are being shortchanged, are searching for something more profound, more holy and more soul-satisfying. Will we be too late at the gate?

For "liberated" priests who are beginning to realize that they also are out in left field, and who feel the urge to return to their Father's house, where may they start and what may they do? Would they perchance take advice from a failure who deliberately walked away from his active priestly vocation? Over the past years, sad experience has taught me some essential basic truths about holiness. I need to be aware of them – perhaps you do too. Let me make them as simple, as palatable, as practical as I am able.

Use the Communion of Saints on earth. For a priest, this means association with other members of the clergy. Initially, selectively seek out and begin to bond with priests easily recognized as sincere seekers of genuine holiness. Form an association with them, meet regularly, take strength from them, and make sure to reciprocate. For a priest's social well-being such associations are vital. Once established, be on the look out to include other needy priests in the group. Encouragement extended to wayward priestly confreres confers great blessings on those priests seeking to pursue holy, priestly lifestyles.

In this diocese there is a small contingent of faithful priests who, for years, have met regularly for prayer, camaraderie and recreation. They also strive to vacation together. Without exception all have remained faithful to the Church and to their priestly duties. I suspect that every diocese contains such pockets of support. All would warmly welcome other priests into their midst. Now, more than ever, sincerely searching for sanctity, priests need the company of similarly minded priests.

Father John McCloskey, a member of Opus Dei and the National Director for the Catholic Truth Society, is a priest for whom I have great admiration. Appearing on the O'Reilly Factor one evening, he stopped the moderator in his tracks when he stated that two essentials for priests are prayer and penance. Some years ago, I had the privilege of having lunch with him in New York City and occasionally have kept in touch with him. This is the type of dedicated man of God to seek out for priestly companionship.

Prayers, and penance even more so, tend to stop not only O'Reilly, but also all of us in our tracks, even priests. Possibly, our problem stems in some degree to what these two P's really mean. Since all love desires union, think of prayer as an act of love that serves as the means of uniting ourselves to God. Through this act of love we are able to touch and embrace the very face of God Himself. Prayer is not always easy but it is spiritually maturing. If prayer has been swept into the corner, why not realistically begin again with only a few prayers. Remember, this is simply the beginning.

The Our Father logically takes center stage. I must confess I have difficulty getting by its first petition. I think of the love and goodness of my own father and gradually ease my meditation over to my heavenly Father and to His infinite love and goodness. The second prayer is the *Morning Offering* in which we offer up to God our prayers, works, joys and sufferings of the entire day. The third prayer is the *Rosary*; for starters, attempt one decade a day, and for twenty days focus attention on one of the major events of our faith each day. In time, this meditation will tend to return to mind time after time as the day progresses. The fourth prayer, which is the favorite of St. Ignatius of Loyola, that has come to be known as the *Suscipe*, says it all. Use it as a benchmark to measure spiritual progress. As your life of prayer improves and expands, ask how comfortably the words and sentiments of this prayer sit with you. These are the words of the *Suscipe*.

Receive, O Lord, all my liberty. Take my memory, my understanding, and my entire will. Whatsoever I have or hold You have given me; I give it all back to You and surrender it wholly to be governed by Your will. Give me only Your love and Your grace, and I am rich enough and ask for nothing more.

How about penance? Don't run off and hide. Every day each of us has ample opportunities to offer up little pains (sometimes large ones), vexations, disruptions, aggravations and disagreeable situations that enter our lives unbidden. Make it a habit to offer these up in union with the sufferings of the Master we have dedicated ourselves to faithfully follow and serve. No hair shirts, no scourges, no pebbles placed in shoes, no four hours of sleep; just steady as she goes – performing ordinary things extraordinarily well.

It would be easy to get carried away and extend this list until it became bewildering and even unmanageable. To repeat, this is a beginning only. God's providence will take care of the rest. These small generous acts of the will are meant to activate the tremendous spiritual supports we received on our ordination day. There is no limit to what God can achieve through his priests.

What rewards will be reaped? Or to put it more bluntly and in unabashedly human terms, you may ask, "What's in it for me?" For starters, as you persist in your efforts to develop a healthy soul through ongoing spiritual exercises, you will awaken one morning and be amazed to discover that your psychoses, neuroses and compulsions have been cut off at their very source. The true meaning of freedom will finally be understood.

TWENTY

Fractures and Structures

No good tree bears bad fruit, nor does a bad tree bear good fruit. Each tree is recognized by its own fruit . . .
  Luke 6: 43–44

Seven years ago, flying in from Toronto on a late Friday evening, I sat next to a businessman. For twenty years he had traveled worldwide expanding his company's business. As we came in over the Thornapple River, the lights from Grand Rapids greeted us. Gazing down, he observed, "In all of my travels, I have never anywhere found a place as nice as this city." In many ways I tend to agree with him – so well situated are we, some twenty miles east of Lake Michigan and midway between the northern Lower Peninsula and the northern border of Indiana.

I don't profess to know either all or even most of the priests in this eleven-county diocese surrounding greater Grand Rapids, but over a fifteen-year period, I have come to have some "feel" for this diocese. Probably, it does not vary a great deal from other episcopal centers throughout the nation. As mentioned elsewhere, Ruth and I have attended Mass in about twenty parishes over the years.

Insight into three occurrences might help to flavor my observations about the diocese. The second time Ruth prepared to go to Confession, soon after entering the Roman Catholic Church, we arrived at Church "A" promptly at 4:00 P.M. The Reconciliation room door was closed and the red light was on. There was a penitent in the room. As we waited, and waited again, we could not help but hear raised voices and laughter coming from this confessional.

Finally, after almost thirty minutes, with no other penitents in church, I knocked gently on the door. The priest confessor opened the door with a surprised look on his face. He had no idea someone was waiting! He and a parishioner were simply sitting there chatting the time away. I decided, since Ruth was a recent convert, this was no place for her and we both left.

The next time we attempted to search out a decent confessor, we visited Church "B," a beautiful old church with the sense of God's presence. As Ruth was completing her confession, the priest advised, "Don't listen to those in Rome. They are just ordinary men who do not have all the answers to the Catholic faith. It is not necessary to always listen to them!"

Then, to add insult to injury, he recommended that Ruth set up an appointment to meet with a Dominican Sister who he considered a good Spiritual Director. [Out of curiosity, with no intent to use her services, I later telephoned the Sister and was told that she charged $60 an hour for her spiritual advice.] Ruth came out of the confessional angry and in tears since she had spent so much time and conscientious effort in learning the faith. I was also angry when I learnt of this misinformation imparted by a bumbling cleric. I reminded her to always distinguish between the Roman Catholic Church and those who falsely profess to be loyal to Rome – to make the distinction between Christianity and Christendom. She recalled this sage advice also given to her by my dear friend, Jerry Urbik.

The devil who never ceases to be active in his constant search for souls, continued in his attempt to lead Ruth away from her hard-won faith. The third attempt took us to Church "C" on the far side of town. Some friend had told us of a great pastor at the parish.

One other couple was waiting for the priest to arrive. This was during Holy Week and the hours for Confession were published in the parish bulletin. At 7:00P.M., the scheduled time to begin, no priest appeared on the scene. At 7:30 P.M., the other couple left. Another fifteen minutes passed by. With feelings of hostility stirring within me, I made my way alone over to a lighted parish center across from the church entrance. The door was unlocked. I made my way in. A group of people was sitting around, talking, laughing, eating cake and drinking coffee. I politely asked where the pastor might be. A man in sports clothes put up his hand and said, "I'm the pastor. Have something to eat!"

Ignoring his hospitality, I asked him about Confessions. He looked surprised, and said, "I've forgotten about them." The assembled group roared with laughter. One of the men spoke up and said, "Who needs Confession?" I silenced him with a glare. He realized I was deadly serious. Suddenly, total quiet enveloped the room.

I addressed my remarks to the pastor, "Father, are you a Sacramental priest?" He answered sheepishly in the affirmative. Whereupon, I said to him, "If so, would you kindly be in the Confessional in five minutes?"

I turned around and walked back to the Church. He appeared two minutes later. As I went into the confessional room, I found it in disarray and needing to be restored to order. Both of us set about arranging the chairs and screen. It was hardly a fitting preparation for this Sacrament of God's great mercy. Ruth was visibly upset and decided not to go to Confession under these uninviting circumstances. The priest advised her, through me, to go home, kneel down and ask Jesus' forgiveness for whatever sins she may have committed. He said there was no need for her to go to Confession. It should cause no surprise to learn that going to Confession has been a source of extreme difficulty for Ruth. However, she is undaunted, offering any discomfort up for the sanctification of priests.

Another Sacrament of Penance episode occurred when my son, Patrick, was home visiting from Los Angeles. We both went to a local church for Saturday afternoon Confession. Since no other penitents were present, the pastor noticed us in Church together. At the end of Patrick's Confession, he made the remark, "Your father is too conservative! He will never find the parish he is searching for." Patrick wondered how a priest could possibly take advantage of the Sacrament of God's forgiveness to downgrade his father to his son.

Let us return briefly to that first Easter Sunday evening when

Jesus, in His glorified body, appeared suddenly to the Apostles in the locked Upper Room. He showed them His hands and side and said, "Peace be with you!" (St. John 20: 21) and then repeated those self-same words. He was about to bestow upon them the great Sacrament leading to peace of mind, soul and body. With that Jesus breathed on them and said, "Receive the Holy Spirit. For those whose sins you forgive, they are forgiven; for those whose sins you retain, they are retained." (St. John 20: 22–23) Why, then, do these American Catholic priests downplay the importance of this Sacrament and its beneficial results by discouraging the faithful from approaching this channel of Divine forgiveness? Some priests spend so little time in the Confessional as ministers of Christ's mercy.

There are perhaps a dozen priests in this diocese in whom I would put my confidence. In some limited cases, I even question the validity of the Masses being offered. The former bishop, aware of these situations through many letters sent to him by observant parishioners, did nothing to bring about needed reform. "Liturgical police" are the descriptive words most often used to disparage and demean the conscientious and concerned letter writers. Much prayer and much patience are needed!

On April 23, 2001, I mailed a letter to the new pastor of Holy Redeemer Church in Jenison to apply for the vacated position of Director of Adult Religious Formation. The letter, containing my qualifications and experience, requested an interview with the pastor. He responded through a telephone call to me on a Saturday morning. The pastor, who prides himself on his organizational capabilities, lost no time getting right to the point. He bluntly stated, "Frank, I am not intending to have an interview with you. I consider you to be divisive. If you tell anyone of this conversation I will simply deny making this statement." Chalk another victory up for the American Catholic Church! Was I surprised? No, it would have been a surprise if he had offered me the position. It was shortly after this conversation that he suddenly was removed from the parish under a cloud. I pray that this self-serving priest will soon come to better understand the essence of the priesthood and return to the full practice of the faith in which he was baptized, confirmed and ordained.

The rejections I received were par for the course. At the public funeral of Mother Teresa, which took place in Calcutta, the sanctuary was awash with archbishops and bishops. There was only one priest with them in the sanctuary whose frail figure was almost lost from view. The following day, at Mother Teresa's private funeral, this same priest was present (there were no bishops at this Mass), along with the Missionaries of Charity, to quietly pray for the soul of this saintly missionary sister. The priest was Father John Hardon, Mother Teresa's Spiritual Director.

During his years of service to our Lord, Father Hardon was never invited to a single session convened by the National Council of Catholic Bishops either in their Washington headquarters or elsewhere. In 1987 he remarked to Dr. Thomas Droleskey that in his considered judgment there were only six bishops in the United States who were totally faithful to the teachings of Christ. There were forty or so who were mostly faithful. The rest of the bishops were dissenters of one variety or another. There are about three hundred and fifty bishops currently in the United States.

The question, then, to be asked is: Why is this defection from authenticity happening? Are there common denominators to which we can point in terms of the root cause of the problem? When I look back over my life, especially the priestly part of it, I am struck by two outstanding factors. The people who have had the greatest effect on my life were men of poverty – poverty of spirit and actual poverty.

Three very special such men have been singled out in this narrative: Father Bill Lane, Arvid Jouppi and Father John Hardon. There are others also. Among them is my Jesuit brother, Father Vincent Morgan. Visiting him one day in the convent/nursing home, where he resides as chaplain to the elderly, I noticed in his closet one sweater and one jacket. He has no interest in personal possessions with one exception – solid good books, including those written by Saint Ignatius of Loyola, G.K. Chesterton and C.S. Lewis, which are treasures indeed. Currently, I have amassed a treasure trove of ten volumes for him all written by Chesterton, given to me by Diane Rose, a dear friend and a fearless defender of the faith, who one day heard me speak of my brother.

I also recall Father Lloyd Ryan, now deceased, who retired to a simple cottage in Cambridge, Ontario. There was a constant flow of visitors to his place for Mass, Confession, prayer and advice. No one was turned away. Some others came, I was informed, to make sure there was enough food in his kitchen. They would bring with them sufficient sustenance to keep his body and soul together.

For years, as a young priest, Father Ryan traveled around the city of Brantford by bicycle, seeing no need for a car. If his cassock became worn and old, he would simply give it an "Irish fix" – a quick touch up with needle and thread. I can't recall seeing him without the beginnings of a smile around the corners of his mouth.

Parishioners have told me that when he was pastor of a small country church, when they were coming home from some early morning party, a light could be seen in the church as they passed by. They knew from experience that he was in there praying for someone in serious need of God's help. Many years ago, I nick-named Father Ryan "the Canadian Cure of Ars." It caused him to chuckle. What a wonderful exemplary priest!

The second common denominator noted in all of these people of God was manliness – a word that comes so easily to mind when thinking of them. What do I mean? I mean men in the real, true sense of the word. The Latin word for man is *vir* from which comes the words virile and virtue – physical and spiritual strength and goodness. Whatever criteria the Vatican uses in its choice of bishops, I dearly wish they would give priority to these two: men with a spirit of poverty which leads them to the practice of actual poverty, men who are manly both physically and spiritually. In other words, no wimps need to apply for these positions.

Perhaps a beginning in episcopal structural improvement could include the following: Bishops, would each of you give some serious consideration to the removal of the title of "Your Excellency"? Similarly, Archbishops, would you give serious thought to the elimination of "Your Grace"? Finally, Cardinals – would you kindly throw overboard the title of "Your Eminence"? While we are on the topic, why not continue the process by eliminating the name "Episcopal Palace" in reference to the place where you reside? Would you not agree that these trappings of royalty should be thrown into the dustbin of history? By all means, keep the title of "Your Holiness" for the pope as befitting the office, not the man! Likewise, dignified church vestments should be maintained as well as impressive altar furnishings since they directly relate to the honor and glory of God.

Poverty should begin from the top down. There is an unfortunate weakness in the human nature of all of us that places the honors we receive for our work and our position above the work itself.

To pursue the same avenue of thought, would you further consider the elimination of limousines and expensive automobiles? Since we are on a roll here, this perhaps could lead to more modest dwellings with less expensive furnishings and fewer sumptuous meals as the order of the day, for clergy of whatever rank. When traveling by air, go coach rather than first class. Please, hand in your country-club memberships and sell your summer cottages! As for vacations, they should be few in number and moderately priced. Avoid, like the plague, recreation resorts and expensive hotels. When convening a meeting with your diocesan priests, hold them in a parish or monastery setting as befits the clerical lifestyle rather than staying at a secular resort site.

By attempting to observe actual poverty, the spirit of poverty should emerge if given the proper internal dispositions. The elimination of unnecessary entrenched paid bureaucrats in both chancery offices and rectories would be a step in the right direction. Volunteers and pious laity involved with various apostolates could easily be made available to carry out these responsibilities.

These recommendations are neither harsh nor negative, but are written as a plea to restore the priesthood to a place of honor and imitation in the hearts and minds of the faithful. Obviously, they are also great cost-savers; monies that could better be put to use in more Christ-centered activities. The story is told about General Booth who founded the Salvation Army. In its infancy, dollars were scarce. The General wished to send a telegram to his leaders throughout the country at Christmas with a message to inspire them. He was aware that a wordier message would be more expensive to send. After much thought, he decided on the use of a single word.

Before continuing this narrative, dear reader, pause and ask yourself: What word would you choose under similar circumstances?

I gave it considerable thought and came up with the word "selflessness." It was not a bad choice. The word General Booth chose was "others." Since then, especially at the beginning of the Lenten season, I have chosen that word as my overall attempt to capture the true meaning of "poor in spirit." I must confess failure many times but try to pick myself up whenever I fall down. It tends also to flavor the same spirit during the rest of the year. I do hope I am starting to get the hang of it.

Our episcopal leaders might look to the example of Joseph Cardinal Ratzinger, Prefect of the Congregation of the Doctrine of the Faith, who lived in the eternal city of Rome and now resides as the elected Pope Benedict XVI. Here we are speaking of one of the Church's greatest theologians. In the past when the summer heat in Rome neared its peak, he took an annual vacation. He would travel back to his old seminary, which also contains lodgings for retired priests. There he spent his days conversing with his clerical friends from the days they were together in the seminary. He also took time to teach the seminarians about the true priestly identity. His quarters were no different from that of the priests and he took his daily meals with priests and students. What an inexpensive, productive and happy way for a bishop to spend a vacation!

To those bishops who rejected the presence of Father John Hardon and his advisory expertise at their deliberations in Washington, convened by the National Council of Catholic Bishops, the following message comes to you from eternity through the writings of this holy priest:

When St. Paul told Timothy to teach the faithful not to become rich he spelled out what is at the root of all the evils of the modern world today. Wrote St. Paul, "We brought nothing into the world, and certainly we can take nothing out; but having food and sufficient clothing, with these let us be content. But those who seek to become rich, fall into temptation and a snare and into many useless and harmful desires, which plunge men into destruction and damnation. For covetousness is the root of all evils and some in their eagerness to get rich, have strayed from the faith and have involved themselves in many troubles.'"(I Timothy 6: 7–10) This is an eloquent commentary on the Seventh and Tenth Commandments. It tells the followers of Christ to avoid more than just stealing. It tells them to avoid an accumulation of money because the love of money is the seedbed of pride and pride is the fountainhead of all sins.

What are some other ecclesiastical structural changes that are badly needed in our materialistic culture today? Let's start from this principle: Saintly bishops help to develop holy priests; holy priests help to develop devout parishioners.

The prime focus of a bishop is to concentrate on becoming a saint through all the sacramental and prayerful means at his disposal, a vertical relationship with God before a horizontal relationship with God's people. The care of his priests must be his second concern, individually and collectively. If the external affairs of the diocese begin to eat into his time, by all means, appoint an auxiliary bishop to look after them – one only. Eliminate the need for many auxiliary bishops. An overabundance of such prelates may well indicate that the diocese is too large and should be divided into two or more.

The head diocesan bishop, not the auxiliary, should see every one of his priests individually at least once a year. I am convinced that such an episcopal fraternal concern would have stemmed the outflow of priests into the secular ranks more than any other factor.

I recall attending a Call to Holiness conference in 1999 where Bishop Bruskewicz of Lincoln, Nebraska was a speaker. I happened to be sitting fairly close to the front of the hall. As he spoke, I found myself not closely listening to what he was saying. Rather, I was observing the man behind the words. You recall the old truism: "Your actions speak so loud I can't hear what you're saying." Over and over in my mind the thought, unbidden, kept recurring, "Had he been my bishop at the time when I considered leaving the priesthood, the fatherly affection

I'm seeing here as he speaks to us, would have made it so easy to approach him for a solution to my priestly temptations. During the three years I spent in Gainesville, Texas, not once did I hear from my bishop. He was a good man, to be sure, but this most important function of being a real spiritual father to his priests was lacking." I have listened to too many priests who have left the active ranks, even after many years, still carrying the scars of episcopal neglect for their welfare.

Priests in the diocese observing their saintly bishop would quickly be influenced and edified. This would be the beginning of their efforts to imitate their spiritual father in Christ. May I also ask bishops to spend daily time hearing Confessions? This sacramental function, neglected by so many today, is probably the most difficult activity for priests to perform – hour after hour sitting in a darkened confessional. And please, for the sake of anonymity and availability, insist on an enclosed and darkened confessional booth. The priest is there to absolve from sin in Jesus' name, not to act as priest-psychologist.

These recommendations represent, of course, only a beginning. A beginning nonetheless is so important. It takes the greatest output of energy to go from a state of inertia to a state of motion. Once the train starts rolling, with God's grace and providence, the most important part of the equation can accomplish wonders. What a profound effect it would have on the faithful! Keep in mind; it has taken almost two generations of concentrated neglect to get us to the present low point. Climbing back up will also take years.

Some ecclesiastical sociologists, reacting to the appalling spiritual desert of the Church in America today have recommended a type of episcopal enforcer, appointed by the Vatican, to visit the various dioceses in the United States with special attention given to improving the caliber of seminaries. I disagree with the concept! Rather, this also should be the responsibility of the bishop in whose diocese the seminary is located. Seminaries should receive frequent, often unannounced, visits from the head of the diocese. It is my understanding that there are still pockets of dissent, disobedience to the Church and lack of discipline in our schools for priests. This is where the manliness factor centered in a bishop is so necessary. He must be a man who cannot be intimidated by self-serving administration or faculty. We need bishops who will immediately react to spiritual problems in their dioceses. If tough decisions must be made, such bishops would be able to come forth with a solution. These should be made on principle rather than on the fear of losing human respect. To keep our bishops properly focused, it might be both wise and prudent to empower at least two members with direct access to Rome to oversee this episcopal activity. My two choices [I'm sure I'm not going to be consulted] are Fathers Joseph Fessio, S.J. and Kenneth Baker, S.J. The first Jesuit is now the provost of Ave Marie University in Naples, Florida; the second Jesuit is the editor of the *Homiletic and Pastoral Review*. On a scale of one-to-ten, both receive double digits.

As I read over the last few pages, I realize that this litany can go on indefinitely. It is not my purpose to set out a complete blue print on how to reconstruct the American Catholic Church back into its Roman Catholic roots. The few recommendations mentioned here are some which are dear to my heart, even as the Roman Catholic priesthood is dear to my heart.

If I have been unduly offensive to anyone in these pages, I ask your forgiveness. I also ask forgiveness from God for gradually taking back from Him over the years of my priesthood all that I had offered to Him on the day of my ordination.

I close this chapter with the words of a well-known, well-admired Jesuit priest, the editor of a great religious publication, the *Homiletic and Pastoral Review*. Father Kenneth Baker, S.J., in his April 2002 editorial, has this message for all of us:

If America were to repent and have a change of heart . . . we would have peace at home and we would not have to worry about highjacked planes and bio terrorism because of Moslem hatred of America. Peace is not the absence of war. Peace comes from doing the will of God and treating others with respect and justice. May God give us a change of heart and the peace that goes with it!

These words poignantly bring back the pleading of the beloved Pope John XXIII asking for *metanoia* – a deep, interior, personal change of heart.

TWENTY-ONE

Remembrances and Predictions

Guard what has been entrusted to your care.
I Timothy 6:20

Without doubt, my most accomplished and highly regarded high school teacher was Patrick Sheridan. He was a strict disciplinarian, a no-nonsense professor who put the fear of both God and Patrick Sheridan into the hearts of every young man in the classroom. Ours was a school of 300 – males only. I recall the comment he made one afternoon, when a classmate dredged up an incorrect answer, "John," he stated, "if a train of thought ever ran through your mind, it would wreck it." Alas, the self-same remark might well be made of me, especially as I strive to set down these observations.

A further instructive final thought concerning Patrick Sheridan comes to mind. He taught English and Mathematics at Cathedral High School until a ripe old age, mellowing only slightly towards the end of his illustrious career. He was distinguished for the fact that no student, no matter how astute, ever totally escaped his ire. At the time of his funeral, St. Patrick's Church was jammed to capacity. Outside the church stood an additional crowd comprised mostly of former students – lawyers, physicians, engineers, priests, teachers, salesmen, office and factory workers. Many had tears in their eyes in memory of this man who expected, and for the most part received, excellence from all of us. Is there a lesson to be learned here?

To return to my mainstream meanderings, I trust our modern social engineers will not take my crystal ball musings into their research labs to dissect and critique. God's providence is the one great imponderable, always to be kept in mind, recognized only when we look back and not at the time it occurs.

I write these words from a place called Gilda's Club, named after Gilda Radner, the popular comedienne who died of cancer. Previously, this building had been a Franciscan monastery with fruit trees and beautiful shrubbery in great abundance. The dwelling slowly deteriorated throughout the 1980s and 1990s. We see here in vivid reality, the destructive influence of the progressive forces seeking to carry out their radical liberal transformation of the Church. The occupants gradually dwindled to a few friars who, seeing the handwriting on the wall, sold and abandoned its run-down premises.

Considerable donated monies and loving planning went into its restoration. Today, it is an oasis, a caring home-away-from-home for those with cancer and those who support both patients and survivors. It boasts a small, but dedicated and competent staff, together with a small army of well over 1,000 volunteers. All combine their considerable talents to keep the place humming for the adults and children with this dread disease. There is an effervescent spirit to the place that inspired Ruth and I to active and enthusiastic participation. "Noogieland," the children's area which takes up a good portion of the lower floor, fairly tugs at one's heart. Upstairs, where I write these words, I hear laughter filtering in through the open door from another room.

* * * *

What observations do I wish to share with you? Let's begin with the crisis in the Catholic Church centered upon clerical sexual scandals.

In my humble opinion, a refocusing would clarify the reality. This is not to downplay the act and the seriousness of sexual abuse of under-aged males. In those cases, where such has indeed occurred, there is a crying need to deal with this tragic problem – immediately and firmly. No hiding, no shuffling from place to place; but open, honest, realistic action. Such clerical abuse demands, both in charity and justice, departure at once from the active ranks of the priesthood through the withdrawal of all priestly faculties and privileges. This does not mean throwing such perpetrators to the dogs. As humanely as possible, they should be assigned to places where the danger of repetition is placed at zero tolerance.

The clerical sexual problems we are witnessing today stem from lowering the disciplinary barriers following Vatican II. Among other tragic consequences that occurred, the effect on seminaries was devastating. To put it delicately, seminaries attracted, if not outright encouraged, candidates who were perceived as less than manly.

We are now seeing the results of that rotten fruit. It is for such a reason that I have hammered away at the need for manly bishops to have the courage to restore these places of priestly preparation to their formerly honored and revered status. The larger problem, then, is with homosexuality rather than with pedophilia. Both are most serious but the former, homosexuality, in terms of the number of occasions, is by far a more serious widespread problem.

There is a high level of probability that this current scandal will be a catalyst that ushers in the formal aspects of a schism that has, in fact, been brewing and festering for almost two generations. Very soon, I rather suspect, the Roman and the American Catholic Churches will officially part company and become two separate, recognizable entities. Will they be fairly split down the middle? Hardly! The American Church will probably take over at least eighty percent of the so-called faithful. The Roman Catholics, in all likelihood, will retain no more than twenty percent – this is a generous optimistic estimate.

Over time, a few years at least, I envision the tide turning with many from the American Church swarming into the Roman ranks. The example of the remnant faithful will be the magnet to attract them back. In the American Church arena, the mix of watered-down Christianity and New Age paganism will attract the weaker and repel the stronger. With married priests, women priests, and a democratic structure, power struggles will inevitably begin soon to occur. This new Church, because of the lack of a legitimate seat of authority, will split into numerous factions, vying with each other for a piece of the power pie.

Obviously, progress in and by itself is in no means to be eschewed. Only when it attempts to confuse freedom (the right to do what we ought, the right to do what we should) and license (the right to do what we want) do problems begin to occur. For all true Catholics, the legitimate seat of moral guidance is found in the 2,000 years of the uncompromising teaching of Roman authority. When moral constraints are disregarded, regression, not progression, is the inevitable result.

It is also my considered opinion that scores of non-Catholics will join the Roman Catholic Church, gradually at first, but then, in ever-increasing numbers. In the space of thirty or forty years, this initially marginalized group will become a recognizable beacon on a hill, bringing about badly needed positive influences on our standards of morality, our culture, and our politics. It will follow the principle of "America is great when America is good."

I don't plan to be around to see this happening but I pray that my children and grandchildren will. Even now, the good soil is in process of being prepared for that day. My dear friend, Father Hardon, had a much better vision than have I. More than once, referring to the Roman Catholic Church, I heard him exclaim, "The twentieth century is the worst century we have ever experienced in the entire history of the world. The twenty-first century will be the greatest."

I am beginning to see the faint glimmerings of that light. It is a recognized phenomenon of democracy that the more godless a nation becomes, the more does government tend to take control over the lives of its citizens. As that multi-tentacle bureaucratic influence begins to recede, we will start to recognize that we are succeeding in our quest for true greatness in America.

To continue with my musings – regarding what has been described as the "religious vocations" crisis, some of it is real, but much of it has been contrived. Those dioceses and religious communities which followed the drum beat of the progressive forces, have deteriorated and diminished in quality of life, numbers and influence. How severe has it become? On excellent first-hand authority, I was informed that the still active but aging

Dominican sisters in Grand Rapids are so busily engaged in their programs of social justice and Eastern mysticism they no longer have the time nor the inclination to visit with aged and incapacitated members of their own community. Their work has taken on such world-shaking importance that it has become necessary to hire lay staff to care for their infirm, formerly dedicated, great teachers of yesteryear. Who, then, in their right mind would wish to join such an order? Once such a vibrant force in Catholic education, it continues to lose its identity.

During a recent discussion with a rather free-wheeling Dominican sister on their diminishing numbers, she acknowledged my observations concerning their concentration on non-religious activities, and made this startling statement, "I am aware that we are a dying order but what a great time we are having in the process!"

By way of comparison, the Missionaries of Charity, founded by Mother Teresa of Calcutta, and the Sisters of Mary, Mother of the Eucharist in Ann Arbor, founded by Mother Assumpta, continue to flourish and thrive, along with several similar religious orders throughout the country who have without compromise maintained their traditional approach to the love and service of God and neighbor. They attract an undiminished flow of new candidates. Theirs is an entirely different type of problem – finding the needed resources to build additional facilities for the large numbers of dedicated women desirous to join them.

Similar communities of men have sprung up to fill the void occasioned by the exodus that began in the 1960s, continuing to this day. The Legionaries of Christ are a typical example; selective in the choice of candidates, demanding in discipline, uncompromising on orthodoxy, they have come to be described as the "new Jesuits." The order has received some unwarranted criticism for the sometime aggressive means employed when seeking excellence in vocations. I see it as a reflection of the dictum: "The nature of goodness is to diffuse itself to others." Compare their zeal in seeking the brightest and the best to that of a segment of the American Catholic Church that advertises for vocations to the priesthood on MTV. It forces one to ask: "Where are they parking their brains?"

There is a new promising phenomenon among some segments of the Dominican order of men. I can't help but think that St. Thomas Aquinas, that great shining light, who is listed among their illustrious members, is focusing his attention from his celestial dwelling in guiding their recent approach. For some years now, I have read of certain vague references to the East Coast Dominicans. Evidently, they decided to return to a thorough study of the Vatican II documents, along with the supporting materials and history associated with that era. Their assiduous research has resulted in a deeper understanding and appreciation of what was truly envisioned for religious priests. Gradually, quietly, they have been assembling all the pieces, taking from pre-Vatican II days what should be maintained, and adding those authentic elements from the Council to produce a cohesive well-formulated entity.

At this juncture, I need to recount an interesting bit of background. For many generations, prior to the mid-1960s, the Dominicans and the Jesuits enjoyed a healthy, respectful, friendly competition. Both were superb teaching orders and the competition inspired both orders to strive to outdo one another. The real winners were the large numbers of well-educated graduating students from their colleges and universities.

How I prayerfully hope that the Jesuits of today would take special notice of the newly formatted Dominican approach, seek to renew a competitive spirit and challenge their former friendly rivals with similar reforms. Do they have the intestinal fortitude to engage in such a battle? As the new Dominicans begin to attract new men to their ranks, as the Legionaries of Christ man the battlements, I pray that a clarion call will go forth from Jesuit leaders, beginning with their Superior General, to once again gird themselves for spiritual battle – this time even against the death-dealing, prideful forces from within their own order.

Imagine if you will the Jesuits, the Dominicans and the Legionaries vying with each other for their place in the sun, all arrayed to do battle against the common enemy of secular materialism. Again, do the Jesuits have the stomach for it? Perhaps a formal challenge from the East Coast Dominicans might get their attention and from that point, with the grace of God, who knows?

*   *   *   *

Finally, one personally important issue: What can be done with the great number of inactive priests who wish to return to the active ranks? In spite of admitted failings, we continue to possess the grace of ordination. The hero in the parable of the Prodigal Son is not the son, but the father. Are there one or two bishops out there with sufficient fatherly concern and loving hearts to walk out with arms wide open to welcome us home again?

Serendipity is understood as discovering or experiencing something of considerable value and, in the process, surprisingly discovering something else of equal or even greater value. Thus, it happened for Ruth and me in January of 2007. We had received a gracious invitation from Jerome (Jerry) Urbik and his dear and charming wife, Barbara, for a weekend visit to their warm and inviting domestic church home in suburban Chicago. It has proven to be an oasis in our heavily charged secular culture for their six children and twenty-six grandchildren. As the saying goes: It was an offer we could not refuse. Long ago, our hosts had placed their lives in the hands of Divine Providence rather than to vague chance.

On Sunday morning prior to our departure for home, we attended an eagerly anticipated Latin Mass at St. John Cantius Catholic Church, recognized for its edifying, soul-satisfying ceremonies and sacred music. The Holy Sacrifice of the Mass, both in English and in Latin, is celebrated with the greatest reverence in a truly prayerful atmosphere. The church building takes one into a different realm – the realm of the sacred. It reminds one of some of the beautiful European churches, untouched by the recent, often barn-like changes. A monument to traditional Catholic architecture and a living museum of sacred art, it was lovingly built in 1893 by Polish immigrants. Attending the Holy Sacrifice of the Mass there was an unforgettable grace-filled experience.

The serendipitous portion of our weekend, though, occurred

a day earlier. Jerry had arranged for me to meet three inactive priests living in the area. (As an aside, it may be of casual interest to note that my full Christian name is Francis (Frank) Joseph and my Jesuit brother's name is Vincent. The names of the three visitors in chronological order are: Joseph, Frank and Vincent.) All three had married following their departures from the ranks of the clergy in the 1970's and 1980's. At the time of our visits, all had retired from successful business careers. Two of the visitors had been diocesan priests, while the third was an order priest – an immensely popular preacher of parish missions and retreats. Subsequent to his departure, the order priest had established his own company; he now employs one hundred plus workers. His wife suffered a stroke and requires his total devoted attention, while his two sons continue to operate his thriving business. The two diocesan priests attend Mass daily at the local parish church; the religious order priest is unable to do so but faithfully attends Mass on Sundays and on prescribed Holy Days of Obligation. All three are gentlemen in the true sense of the word. All three are solidly Roman Catholics.

In the course of our conversations they informed me of a local bishop who sent invitations to all known inactive priests in his diocese to a special gathering. Since it was the bishop taking the leadership role, a surprisingly large number attended, including the two diocesan priests. It proved to be heart-warming and healing with plans to hold future such sessions. Even though all three priests have left their active ministries over twenty-five years ago, I asked each one how they would respond to an episcopal invitation to become more actively engaged in their diocese. Their responses were immediate: "In a heartbeat," "In a blink of an eye," and "I would if I could."

Upon returning home, I began pondering the possibilities to the point of inviting two astute diocesan canon lawyers to our home for lunch and open dialogue. (Come to think of it, aren't all canon lawyers astute?) Both were open to the possibilities of inactive priests' involvement. These are but a few observations that surfaced.

In 2005 there were approximately 42,000 active priests nationwide, a twenty-five percent decline since 1965 – 10,500 priests left the active ranks during that period. Without getting into extrapolations, permutations or actuarial tables, there must be on a conservative estimate over 8,000 inactive priests today still alive in our national midst. If Rome responded favorably to a limited ministry, there could well be a minimum of 1,000 plus candidates who would respond with an *ad sum* – here I am!

A cautionary consideration – in those dioceses containing a preponderance of activist clerics pressing for a married clergy, it might be prudent to inform them that any effort to use this "coming home apostolate" to further their personal ends – a married clergy – would only tend to scuttle the entire episcopal effort.

Returning priests to active clerical activity should assist as volunteers – without pay. However, inactive priests who may wish to return and who are financially comfortable but due to whatever circumstances, are unable to make this transition, might be inspired to subsidize the meager earnings of less afflu-ent men seeking to make an active contribution. I can envision many apostolates for such returning priests, but who am I to sec-ond-guess a bishop as to where these volunteer "reverts" might do the most good for the sanctification and salvation of souls.

Allow me to put my toe in the water in this next step. Everything I read concerning Pope Benedict XVI only serves to increase my love, respect and admiration for our beloved Holy Father. On October 18, 2006, he addressed the bishops of west-ern Canada during their *ad limina* visit to Rome. These are his words:

I wish, therefore, to commend your promotion of the Sacrament of Penance. While this Sacrament is often considered with indifference, what it effects is precisely the fullness of healing for which we long.

A new-found appreciation of this Sacrament will confirm that time spent in the confessional draws good from evil, restores life from death and reveals anew the merciful Face of the Father.

"Fullness of healing . . . good from evil . . . restores life from death . . . merciful Face of God." These effects derived from Confession are assuredly for the good of penitents. However, they also grace the priest who administers this Sacrament of mercy and peace. May I tread on sacred, sacramental territory for a moment? What is written here is stated under strict obedience to the Church in its discipline and practice. Given the proven worth of select priests returning to active ministry, may it become a hope that a petition for the faculty to hear Confessions could be sent to Rome. This unanswered question I humbly place in the hands of God's loving and divine providence.

The following prayer of Saint Therese of Lisieux is for all priests: those who have remained constant and faithful, and those who have strayed into whatever path, that God's grace may penetrate our souls to the very core of our being.

Jesus, Eternal Priest, keep your priests within the shelter of your Most Sacred Heart, where none can touch them. Keep unstained their anointed hands, which daily touch your Sacred Body. Keep unsullied their lips daily tinged with your Precious Blood. Keep pure and unworldly their hearts, sealed with the sublime mark of the priesthood. Let your Holy Love surround and protect them from the world's contagion. Bless their labors with abundant fruit, and may the souls to whom they minister be their joy and consolation here, and their everlasting crown in the hereafter. Amen.

TWENTY-TWO

Bishops Are People Too

Guard the good deposit that was entrusted to you – guard it with the help of the Holy Spirit who lives within us.
    II Timothy 1:14

Throughout many of the preceding pages, I, who turned my back and deliberately walked away from the active priesthood through my own selfishness, have had little right to include my observations. The severest critics in ancient Israel were the holy prophets who loved God's chosen people most. I'm not even close to being in their league. Do I offer my observations because, through the grace of God, the sacred priesthood is, in truth, my lost love? I sincerely hope so!

A few years ago, a priest exclaimed to me, "Our diocese is in open revolt against our current bishop." What advice might I dare offer to an incoming episcopal leader? I volunteer these words for all bishops, as well as for priests. By no means are they comprehensive; they represent only a few doable, necessary activities. Keep in mind that my perspective, wider than most, comes from more than 60 years within and without the active priesthood – both sides of the altar.

Every bishop should begin every day of his ministry with a vision that is both broad and encompassing! I can think of no better focus than the honor and glory of God and the sanctification and salvation of souls. The place to begin must be with the bishop himself.

Early in the 20th century, *The London Times* proposed a contest. The newspaper asked people to submit essays on the topic: What Is Wrong With the World? Gilbert Keith Chesterton decided to respond to the challenge. Giving the question some deep thought, he submitted his essay consisting of one word. That one word was: "Me."

It is unfortunate that the prayer of praise at the beginning of Mass known as the *Gloria* has received such a poor English translation – "Glory to God in the highest and peace to his people on earth." Correctly, it should read, "Glory to God in the highest and peace on earth to men of good will." Who among mankind are people of good will? It refers to those who first make an act of the will to reach out to authentic truth and goodness. God, always the perfect gentleman, waits for that "good will" effort from us before His grace floods our souls.

What has this to do with clerical advice? What a feeling of presumption I am experiencing as I write these words! However, I am prompted to launch out into the deep. Bishops especially should be mindful that they have been given the fullness of priestly power, bestowed upon them by none other than Jesus, the First Priest. These gifts are not for their own glory or aggrandizement; they are to be used exclusively for the honor and glory of God and for the good of souls.

Even I, an inactive priest, have sensed that pouring forth of wisdom, understanding, knowledge, counsel, fortitude, piety and fear of the Lord upon making that initial act of my will. I vividly recall the occasion when I was invited to attend a meeting of the inactive priest/members of Call to Action, along with their wives. I prayed fervently while I was driving to the parish that was hosting the meeting. I had asked Ruth to remain at home since I was unsure of what the evening might offer. Indeed, our former, now retired, bishop was the guest of honor.

The first hour was filled with hospitality, good will and merriment. Following an excellent meal, each of the twenty-nine persons present, husbands and wives, was requested to offer a few words of inspiration and encouragement. I listened intently to statements about some who regularly hired themselves out to parishes to celebrate Mass, in order to give pastors a break. I was deluged with remarks concerning the downside of celibacy, the need for married and women priests, and the rights of women over their own bodies concerning artificial contraception and the power of reproduction through terminating a pregnancy. Some spoke of how they would celebrate with joy the news of the death of Pope John Paul II . . .

I was third or fourth from the last person to speak. I stood up and, it seemed, with no effort, and certainly with no fear, spoke in defense of Roman Catholicism, the greatness of John Paul II, the grace of celibacy, the heresy which would allow women priests, the difference between freedom and license as related to contraception and abortion. I finally sat down to be greeted with total silence. It was then that the wife of the priest sitting next to me leaned over and whispered words that I will never forget, "I don't agree with everything you said; but I certainly admire your courage for saying what you did."

I took no credit. Driving home afterwards, I knew that it was God's grace working through me. Before the meeting, I had asked Mary to obtain for me the strength from her divine Son not to betray Him a second time. You may ask, "Why Mary?" It is what Catholics describe as intercessory prayer. It is interesting that many Protestant groups are beginning to utilize this type of devotion. As I drove along I recalled that the first miracle took place at a wedding feast and it was through Mary that Jesus performed his first "sign." Thus it was that I asked her to again go to her Son to transform the water of my fear into the wine of courage. Jesus answered my prayer in spades!

Dr. Laura Schlessinger, the well-known radio personality who often enlightens callers on her program, will frequently end the conversation with the words, "Now, go and do the right thing!" She informs them not to go and do what they might want to do but rather what they should do, what they ought to do. Here we have the proper mix of truth and goodness. It fits in perfectly with the definition I once read of happiness: "the consciousness of a perfect act." It means accepting this particular objective truth, no matter how unpalatable or difficult, and then putting it into action through a deliberate act of will. Is it a pleasurable exercise? Quite frequently, "No!" Does it result in an inner awareness of personal satisfaction? Decidedly, "Yes," due to the happy marriage of truth and goodness. Does everyone like Dr. Laura? By no means! People frequently remark: "She's a trouble-maker! She's divisive! (Substitute the words "counter cultural" in place of divisive.) She makes me feel uneasy, fearful, uncomfortable!" In spite of these negative connotations, if you asked the question: Is she respected?, the answer is a resounding, "You bet she is!"

Has Dr. Laura taken hits for her courageous stand? She certainly has, and then comes back for more. Why? Because this Jewish lady never waters down her principles or advice! Rather than lower the bar, she consistently attempts to raise people up to a higher ethical level of conduct. I have heard her chide Catholics for not knowing what their faith really teaches. She urges them to borrow or buy a copy of the *Catechism of the Catholic Church* to read, study, absorb and appreciate. She has read it twice, extols its wisdom and refers to it as a "noble" work.

My son, Patrick, on a visit from California, informed me that both he and his Los Angeles buddies describe me as eccentric and all make it a point to visit us at his home when Ruth and I are on the west coast. I look forward to our friendly crossing of swords. When next we meet, their perception will be corrected when I inform them that I am not eccentric but counter-cultural, as a fearless defender of Roman Catholicism recently reminded me. At that point another great discussion will ensue – ten against one, but they don't have a ghost of a chance. I can hardly wait to "slay" them, one after another.

Every bishop and priest worth his salt, especially today, should be seen as counter-cultural. To all my clerical confreres – resist with all your might the temptation to succumb to our pagan culture – rather, inspire those who may be floundering, lift them up with your words of encouragement and, especially, through your example.

If such graces are given to an inactive priest, imagine the out-pouring of supernatural assistance for bishops of good will. St. Ignatius of Loyola stated it so well, "There are few men who realize what God would make of them if they would abandon themselves entirely into His hands and let them be formed by His grace." So, bishops, ask yourselves the questions: Do I want to be liked? Do I describe myself as a moderate – Catholicism "lite" – or do I want to be respected for my firm foundation on Roman Catholicism? If the former, it will be business as usual. If the latter, God's superhuman strength will be lavished upon you.

Bishops, please encourage your priests to spend twenty minutes before every daily Mass, in an enclosed, sound proof, darkened confessional. By way of a personal observation, I would assign all reconciliation rooms to oblivion.

If, at first, no one approaches the confessional, be patient and use the time of waiting to begin the recitation of your Divine Office. Word will get around, God will look after this. The Cure of Ars also spent time in prayerful and patient waiting for the floodgates to gradually open into a torrent. Write about your convictions on the blessings derived from frequent Confession in the pages of your official diocesan Catholic newspaper.

Continuing for a moment with the Sacrament of Confession, please choose a personal top-notch Spiritual Director – a manly, no nonsense, truly holy priest for your weekly personal encounter with God's mercy. Similarly, arrange for every single priest in your diocese to be supplied with a choice of Spiritual Directors. You may wish to select and recruit them from among your retired priests.

Bishops, I am aware of no diocese without dissident priests (heretics) today. Dissent has become so rampant that in Grand Rapids we have a pastor who publicly termed himself the "happy heretic." Do not despair or become discouraged.

Years ago, the brilliant Anne Muggeridge wrote an article on dealing with this problem. Take time to determine who are the leading dissenters among your parish priests. Invite three or four of them in separately for a fatherly chat. Remind each priest of the day of his ordination when he promised obedience to the bishop of the diocese. Ask him then if he will again promise that obedience to you. If the answer is yes, request that he remove himself from all further dissent in both words and actions – spell out in detail what specifically they are. Inform him of your prayers and support. Request a second meeting within a month to review his cooperation. If, at that time, there is indication of an honest effort on his part to reform his life, then continue to work with him and appoint a solid Spiritual Director to assist him.

If your request for obedience is either refused or disregarded, ask him to pray and think about it for forty-eight hours. If, by then, he continues to refuse to obey you, ask him to pack his belongings and leave the rectory within three days. In all likelihood his refusal to obey indicates that poverty and chastity have also been breached. The penalty of those priests who cavort with the world and the flesh is that they never grasp the joy of the spiritual. Be kind but firm and always strive to listen to the priest's story first, and provide a fatherly offer to help him with his problems. Word will quickly spread among the clergy and a degree of "peace in the valley," as well as a rise in clergy morale, not experienced for many years, will become noticeable. Priests will come to realize they have a leader who genuinely loves both them and the Church they are dedicated to serve.

Father, as you daily offer up the Holy Sacrifice of the Mass, do so with the utmost reverence of body, mind and will – hands folded in prayer, eyes concentrated on the altar, prayers uttered with attention and devotion. Make each gesture an act of your deep faith and love. On a personal note, I am convinced a serious error occurred when both the altar and the priest were turned around to celebrate Mass facing the people. It became a closed circle in which those present gradually came to celebrate themselves. The result has been that the essential sacrificial nature of the Mass has been de-emphasized in favor of the Mass as a meal.

On good authority we read of the emphasis that Abraham Lincoln placed on the final words of the *Gettysburg Address*. He emphasized not "of" or "by" or "for" but rather the word "people" – three times over. There is a similarity in an important but often overlooked prayer in the Mass. Prior to standing for the recitation of the *Lord's Prayer*, the celebrant (not the parishioners) recites or chants the prayer which sums up the sacrificial action of the Eucharist: "Through Him, with Him, in Him, in the unity of the Holy Spirit all glory and honor is yours, Almighty Father, forever and ever." I have heard only one scholarly priest who properly emphasizes this beautiful prayer of praise.

I often suspect this lack of attention is due to the unautho-rized, distracting, touchy-feely excitement in anticipation of holding hands, or assuming the *"orans"* posture of the priest as the congregation stands to recite the *Our Father*. Again, the Mass is not a community celebrating itself but the Christocentric Sacrifice of God's Son to His heavenly Father. The laity partici-pates in this solemn act of profound adoration by symbolically placing their lives on the paten and in the chalice. They offer up their very selves in union with the Son to His Father and to theirs. God in turn rewards the offering by giving them the ines-timable gift of His Son's glorified Body, Blood, Soul and Divinity in Holy Communion.

Since the Blessed Sacrament is the central reality in our wor-ship, encourage the establishment of chapels of adoration throughout your diocese. Make certain your parish priests par-ticipate in these hours of adoration along with the devout mem-bers of the faithful.

This list could go on much longer: Use altar boys rather than altar girls to encourage vocations. Give primacy of place to Gregorian chant. Eliminate the nine-to-five schedule of office hours for your priests and insist that they do not live apart from the rectory. Clean up some of the wretched catechetical pro-grams in your schools. Eliminate the invasion of the altar by extraordinary Eucharistic ministers. Guard against the femi-nization of the Church by encouraging and training a few good men to act as lectors. Train only qualified instructors who know and practice their faith to instruct others in the RCIA program (Rite of Christian Initiation of Adults). Where does one stop? Rather, where does one begin? What is written here is only a beginning.

A bishop who removes his rose-colored glasses, and serious-ly asks to what degree Christ lives and reigns in the minds and hearts of his priests and people, will find the answer is shocking and disturbing. In all societies and places, Christianity to some degree has been influenced by the prevailing culture. Today, we are awash and wallowing in, inundated by, a culture that is pleasure-driven, absorbed by the quest for financial security, undeniably driven by technology and consumerism. Rather than being set apart, Christianity in America appears to be attempting to raise the bar of secular materialism.

The saintly, perceptive, blind Jesuit retreat master, who preached to us in the seminary years before the advent of the sexual revolution of the 1960s, made the comment, "Paganism and nudity go hand in hand." His comment gives us pause to ponder how deeply today we have descended into a society that is zealously attempting to relegate God to the sidelines and from there to irrelevance.

Recall how I reacted when asked to assemble a plan to turn Aquinas College back into a Catholic institute of higher learning. I remembered the adage, "Never send a boy to do a man's job." In consequence, I contacted three outstanding and successful educators associated with Catholic colleges and universities.

A strong recommendation is made to bishops to act in the same manner. The outstanding members of the episcopacy, I suggest without reserve, are Bishop Fabian Bruskewicz of , Nebraska; Archbishop Charles Chaput of Denver, Colorado; Archbishop John Myers, recently from Peoria, Illinois, and now in Newark, New Jersey; and Bishop Thomas Olmsted from Phoenix, Arizona. It will be time well spent to consult with these manly, solidly orthodox prelates.

A devout priest friend of mine, who was the chaplain of a Carmelite monastery, spent much time in the company of Our Lord in the Blessed Sacrament. After years of faithful service, he left this diocese to be accepted into the Diocese of Lincoln, Nebraska. A couple of months after being assigned to a parish, he telephoned me and remarked that the move was much like going to heaven. What a priestly tribute to his great bishop!

Above all, don't give way to despair! It took Father Michael Scanlan, President of Franciscan University of Steubenville, fourteen years to turn the college from a party school to an outstanding university of higher learning. Episcopal fears have led to silence, including fear of feminists with their agenda to restructure the Church in their image; fear of all segments of the secular media and some segments of even the religious media; fear of controversy which might lead to confrontation create a paralyzing environment. Added to these fears are the besetting issues of moral and cultural relativism resulting from our misguided pursuit of multiculturalism.

How very difficult it must therefore be for a bishop who has heard over and over again "Yes, Father" and "yes, your Excellency" for twenty-five or thirty years, to come to terms with dissent. Such fears are real; such fears are daunting! How much these present day successors of the apostles who strive to carry out their mission need our prayers, our support and our encouragement.

Again, a bishop must begin with himself to use all the spiritual armor available to him. His second focus must be on his priests, collectively and individually. Insist, Bishop, on arranging your schedule to spend an hour with every priest in your diocese at least once a year – more frequently with priests you perceive as troubled. Be fatherly to each of them – kind but firm. At the end of every priestly meeting, request the priest to kneel down and renew his pledge of obedience to you.

It then becomes the main province and responsibility of the priests to reach their parishioners. Supply your parish priests with ample materials to effectively carry out their sacramental, pastoral and preaching duties.

Bishops, to directly contact the lay people of the diocese, earnestly endeavor to perform the Sacrament of Confirmation personally rather than delegate this authority to pastors. What an opportunity to begin an ongoing systematic, organic presentation of Catholic beliefs and practices. As a follow-up, each of your challenging Confirmation sermons might be summarized in the official diocesan newspaper for the edification of the entire diocese.

I vividly recall Pope John Paul II appearing on the balcony for the first time above St. Peter's Square. I feel his opening message to the world; "Do not be afraid" was truly emblematic of his own priesthood. Would that every bishop could write those words on his tombstone!

Epilogue

If, when I was in my twenties, thirties or forties, the question was asked of me: "Would you rather be liked or respected, if given the choice?" I am certain I would have taken time to ponder my answer. Today, as I do my best to prepare for my final journey, the question is a no-brainer. Respect, by all means! In fact, I often jokingly make the observation that I am very even-tempered – always angry.

You see, the marks of the priesthood are indelibly with me, thanks to God's love and mercy. As soon as I "launch out into the deep," all those priestly graces inundate me. The same is true for those manly clerics who step forward in faith. Immediately, they are surrounded with supernatural fortitude or courage.

Sometimes, in somewhat of a moment or two of heroic idealism, for whatever reason I recall the play of *Cyrano de Bergerac*, the super swordsman with his mellifluous tongue and prominent proboscis. As the tale winds down, having been set upon by a band of brigands without warning in cramped quarters, he is severely wounded and realizes that death is near. He makes his way to Roxanne, now living in a convent. Standing upright, rapier in hand, *engarde* against whatever enemy might lurk, human or devilish, and determined to die with the unsullied white plume in his hat and with his boots on. And, I whisper to myself, "Saint Joseph, patron of a happy death, pray for me!"

Some years ago, God willed to give me a gift to knock some of the rough spots from me. Long ago I came to the point of thanking Him daily for my myasthenia gravis. It is with tongue in cheek when I inform others that this disease only affects very brilliant and very wealthy people. It has been described as a minor league type of Lou Gehrig's disease since it attacks the autoimmune system causing some paralysis about the eyes, mouth and throat in conjunction with extreme fatigue. In the past year the symptoms have become more pronounced. This disease, however, is not anywhere near the category of cancer, a stroke or a heart attack – so God is certainly gentle with me. Has it brought me closer to Him by giving me the grace to share slightly in His passion? It certainly has! I pray more fervently and no longer rush about. I refer to this gift from God as the "Elmer Fudd Syndrome." When my tongue becomes extremely tired (telling me that I am talking too much) the paralysis sets me up for my imitation of Elmer hunting Bugs Bunny – You cwazy wabbit! All of us should try to get serious over bringing a healthy genuine sense of humor into our lives and in the process come to view ourselves in a laughable light. It sure helps to smooth out the bumps in the road which all of us inevitably encounter. This little gift from God has caused me to begin my day with three short prayers as soon as I awaken.

- Adoration: *I adore Thee, O Christ, and I praise Thee, because by Thy Holy Cross, Thou hast redeemed the world.*
- Mercy and Forgiveness: *O Lord Jesus Christ, Son of the Eternal Father, have mercy on me a poor sinner.*
- Trust and Complete Confidence in God's Loving Providence: *God the Father, God the Son and God the Holy Spirit, this day I beseech Thee for the grace to fully acknowledge Thy supreme dominion over me and my total dependence upon Thee.*

Is prayer efficacious? Recently, when a surgeon split my sternum to remove my thymus gland in order to alleviate my myasthenia gravis symptoms, I remember not five seconds when I worried about the procedure.

To bring closure to my story, I began with Bishop Kevin Britt. Following his death, it must have been a year or more we awaited the appointment of a new diocesan leader. Finally, Bishop Walter Hurley arrived to take over the episcopal reins. As of this writing, he has been in our midst for well over a year. The jury is still out and I pray daily that he will not simply rearrange the deck chairs on the Titanic. Once the dust had settled and he was into a regular routine, I mailed him a letter informing him of my background, my encouraging meeting with Bishop Britt and my desire to assist with wayward priests. After all, was I not one of them? His letter now seems edged in black arrived some two weeks later from the Vicar General, his so-called alter ego. In effect it stated, "Thanks for your offer – have a good day." Ouch! Then, instinctively, the short prayer to the three Persons of the Blessed Trinity surfaced; serenely I became aware that everything was in God's providential care.

It is with great reluctance that I bid you goodbye. May the love of the Sacred Heart of Jesus and the Immaculate Heart of Mary be always in our minds and in our hearts.

This Is My Friend
Let me tell you how I made His acquaintance
I had heard much of Him, but took no heed.
He sent daily gifts and presents, but I never thanked Him.
He often seemed to want my friendship, but I remained cold.
I was homeless, and wretched, and starving and in peril
every hour; and He offered me shelter and comfort and
food and safety but I was ungrateful still.
At last He crossed my path and with tears in His eyes
He besought me saying, "Come and abide with me."

Let me tell you how He treats me now.
He supplies all my wants.
He gives me more than I dare ask.
He anticipates my every need.
He begs me to ask for more.
He never reminds me of my past ingratitude.
He never rebukes me for my past follies.

Let me tell you further what I think of Him.
He is as good as He is great.
His love is as ardent as it is true.
He is as lavish of His promises as He is faithful in keeping them.
He is as jealous of my love as He is deserving of it.
I am in all things His debtor, but He bids me call Him Friend.

From an old manuscript

Afterword

David Morgan

My dad passed away on February 24, 2008, from complications of Myasthenia Gravis. He worked up to his last day in a small part-time job to keep himself occupied. His job as a Heavenly Ham/HoneyBaked Ham Consultant afforded him the opportunity to do what he loved best, connecting with other people. He used his unique "Gift of the Blarney," as we Irish say, to get to know them. My brother Patrick's friends, as well as mine, said at Dad's funeral that he made them feel like they were a part of our family because of the care and interest he took when talking with them. On more than one occasion we warned our friends, "Remember, when you meet Dad, expect the third degree!" Dad always asked questions of those who entered our house. They weren't superficial questions but questions that made you look deep within yourself for the answers. Questions that made you think: Where AM I going? What DO I want to do?

As I sit here thinking over the months that have passed since Dad died, I still wonder to myself those very same questions. However, those questions have changed, slightly, but importantly. Where am I going, without my father's wisdom and guidance? What do I want to do, without my father's influence and suggestions? These questions underline the profound effect my Dad had on my life, as well as my brother's. Every major decision I made, I asked my Dad's thoughts on it. The same can be said about Patrick. We didn't always do what he suggested, but we did ask his opinion on things.

I can remember back to May of 1995, when I had decided

that I was going to ask Stacey to be my bride. We had only known each other for a few short months, but I had made a decision. So, I asked my Dad about it. He and my Mom sat me down for a talk, and at the end I was given their blessing. All through my life, I looked to my parents for their wisdom and guidance. They looked to their Heavenly Father for guidance as well. If more children looked to parents, as well as their Heavenly Father for guidance, I believe that many of our social ills would be nonexistent.

My mother, as his wife, said that she felt she could share everything with him. And in turn receive his open and honest appraisal of any situation she faced. Various topics and shared interests were discussed thoroughly. They particularly enjoyed watching Jeopardy and played against each other, holding hands to the last. Dad always tried to stretch our minds and learn new things, enjoying the challenge and experience of it.

My Dad never gave up, never backed down, and always tried to do what was right, honest, and moral. When I was a child growing up, we visited a large restaurant chain for dinner. Before our meal arrived a waitress spilled an entire pot of hot coffee on Dad's lap. He went to the bathroom to check out the damage done, and then we left the restaurant to go home for some in-house first aid. My mother realized that he had suffered second-degree burns and needed to go to the hospital where he was packed with ice. My parents were informed that he could have sued the restaurant, but instead he chose to be compensated with $3000.00 and a free meal for the family. Without batting an eye, my Dad instructed us to "order up to the hilt." We even got dessert! His humor was what carried him through trying times like this. That is the sort of person my father was; his solution was a far cry from the million-dollar hot coffee suits that occur today.

Dad's quiet example of perseverance was also a large factor in my life. He never gave up; he always continued ahead. It wasn't always the smoothest or straightest of paths, but he kept putting one foot in front of the other. In October of 2006, in order to help combat his Myasthenia Gravis, my father had to have his thymus gland removed. After the operation he was put in a recovery room and was told he was to be moved to a general room in the morning. Unaware that he was to be pushed in a wheel chair, he got out of bed, took his IV pole, walked down the hall to the elevator, went up to the floor he was to be assigned, walked down a long hall to his room, and sat down in the chair, without any help from anyone. The nurse said that she had never seen anyone walk to their room after an open chest operation. My father was eighty-two years old at this time.

I believe that all who knew my father, either in person or through his writings, feel the loss of his presence. All of us will remember the example and lesson that he left us. Never give up, keep on trying, and always look to God for the answer. As my father would say, "Onward and upward."

APPENDIX A

Twenty-five Ways to Spend an Hour with Jesus

1. Slowly read Sacred Scripture with an attentive heart for God to speak.
2. Recite the Rosary and meditate upon the mysteries.
3. Let God gaze upon you and fill you with His loving presence.
4. Share with Him something that fills your heart with joy and then listen.
5. Share with Him what you are afraid of and then listen.
6. Tell Him what angers you and seek serenity.
7. Speak to Him about your loved ones.
8. Offer up a prayer for an enemy.
9. Discuss your work with Him and seek guidance.
10. Sing a song for Him in your heart.
11. Deepen your commitment to Him by making acts of faith, hope and love.
12. Imagine Mary sitting beside you and praying with you.
13. Renew your loyalty to His Church.
14. Lean on Him and share with Him the burdens of your heart.
15. Thank Him for the Sacraments, especially the Eucharist and Confession.
16. Confess to Him your sins and failures with a sincere heart.
17. Slowly recite the Beatitudes.
18. Pray one Our Father slowly and meditate on its words.
19. Recite one Hail Mary slowly and ponder its rich meaning.

20. Make a profession of faith by reciting the Creed.
21. Pray to the Lord of the Harvest for more vocations to the priesthood and consecrated life.
22. Seek guidance on what the Lord wants you to do with your life.
23. Reflect upon your many talents and gifts and thank Him.
24. Pray for peace in the world.
25. Simply rest in His presence.

APPENDIX B

Appeal to Aquinas College – May 19, 1994

1. Definition of a Catholic College:
   A Catholic University/College, as Catholic, informs and carries out its research, teaching and all other activities with Catholic ideals, principles and attitudes as they are expressed and defined in the Apostolic Constitution *Ex Corde Ecclesiae*.
2. How serious are you?
3. Does the Board of Trustees unanimously share your views?
4. Do you have a Mission Statement? Does it reflect the tenets of *Ex Corde Ecclesiae*?

*   *   *   *

1. Do you have a faculty contract? Does it contain a "duty" clause?
2. Do you have a separate incorporation agreement?
3. Board of Trustees: Its composition, its liability.

*   *   *   *

1. Is Aquinas experiencing financial problems? If so, are they related to alumni support?
2. How does the alumni react to the concept of "Catholic College"?
3. How does public aid (capital funding and/or operational funding) impact and influence you Catholic identity?

4. What percentage of your total funding is received from the state and federal governments?

*   *   *   *

1. Describe your academic staff and departments related to religion and academic excellence in terms of training, competence and experience.
2. Administrative Staff (as above)
3. Support Personnel Staff (as above)
4. Tenure:
Full-time
Part-time
5. Questionnaire for Staff and Support Personnel:
   - Do you support Pope John Paul II?   Yes / No
   - If yes, would you describe your support:
     Very strong / Strong / Strong enough
   - Do you believe priests should marry?   Yes / No
   - Do you believe women should be ordained?Yes / No
   - Do you support traditional Catholic teaching on:
         Sexual morality?   Yes / No
         Humanae Vitae?   Yes / No
         Homosexuality?   Yes / No
   - Do you go to Sunday Mass regularly?   Yes / No
   - Do you attend Mass on Holy Days?   Yes / No
   - Are you Pro-Choice or Pro-Life?
6. Student Body: Describe
7. Is a minimum of 12 semester hours of Thomistic Philosophy taught to all undergraduate students including:
   - Philosophy of the Human Person
   - Ethics
   - Metaphysics
   - Epistemology
   (Preferably in the above order to offset relativism, subjectivism and skepticism)
8. Is a minimum of 12 semester hours of Catholic Theology (not religions studies) taught to all undergraduate students, including:
   - Articles of Faith

- History of Catholicism
- Old and New Testaments
- Sacraments of Liturgy
- Moral Theology and Spirituality

9. Are Catholic beliefs taught in other areas of the curriculum? (Note: If you are earnest about your faith, you cannot compartmentalize it. It weaves through everything you do!)
10. Do you have a Campus Chaplain/Spiritual Director? If so, describe.
11. Do you have requirements for the moral and religious education of all students?
12. What are your campus spiritual activities and resources?
13. Are the students being religiously challenged? This does not mean "are they encouraged to challenge religion?" The timid walk in crowds, the brave in single file!
14. What problems and opposition do you foresee in the pursuit of your goals?
15. Who is your competition?
16. How does Aquinas advertise and promote?

APPENDIX C

RECOMMENDED SPIRITUAL READING

For stability of both priests and laypersons, the importance of spiritual reading cannot be overstated. In fact, without it, a solid interior life of prayer and union with God is simply impossible. It is as necessary for the health of the soul as food is for the body. No spiritual reading equals an absence of sanctity. Such neglect by a priest will cause him to lose his ability to effectively be a spiritual director for the members of his flock – the blind leading the blind. The following recommendations may catch your attention.

First and foremost is the *Imitation of Christ* by Thomas à Kempis, the most widely read spiritual work after the Bible. *This Tremendous Lover* by Dom Eugene Boylan, immensely popular during my seminary days. For one properly disposed, it will lead to an increase in faith, hope, charity, humility and submission to the will of God. *Christ, The Life of the Soul* by Blessed Columba Marmion concerning which Cardinal Mercier, a wholly and brilliant clergyman working in the Vatican made the statement: "Dom Columba makes one touch the face of God." *Treatise on the Love of God* by St. Francis de Sales is a veritable history of God's infinite love for His creatures. *The Soul of the Apostolate* by Dom Chautard is a book that the saintly Pope Pius X described as his "bedside book." *Self-Abandonment to Divine Providence* by Father J. P. Caussade goes to the very heart of all Catholic spirituality, namely, accepting and carrying out the Will of God in our lives. *The Passion and the Death of Jesus Christ* by St. Alphonsus Liguori states: "All the saints cherished a tender devotion toward Jesus Christ in His passion." In *True Devotion to Mary* by Grignon de Montfort, we recognize Jesus as our pattern for living and Mary, His Mother, as the perfect human model. Here we perceive her in her true role leaving us to her Son, along with the beautiful *Magnificat* that she uttered on the occasion of her visit to her cousin Elizabeth; her two other utterances come to us down through the centuries, "Be it done unto me according to Thy word and do whatever He tells you."

This list is simply a basic beginning to assist us in overcoming the secular influences in today's world. To this list, let me add one more saintly person, now deceased, whose cause is up for canonization. Through the grace of God I had the privilege of working with him on a number of projects over a twelve-year period. His name is Father John A. Hardon, s.J. I whole-heartedly recommend everything he wrote!

INDEX